John G[odber]
Play[s]

D0933246

Bouncers, Happy Families, Shakers

Bouncers: 'Simply spellbinding. This is partly because of John Godber's writing with its meticulous social observation that invokes whole life styles with a few lines of dialogue. There's also an unusual insight into the darker, closed world of the bouncers themselves . . . A show that's worth braving any front of house, however formidable.' *Guardian*
'The imagination of author John Godber, his talent for observation and the caricaturing of tricks of behaviour are given ideal form . . . No zoologist could have observed his quarry with greater care or with a greater sense of the grotesque . . . highly satisfying and amusing.' *Scotsman*
'Godber's nightmarish, scatological vision of working-class urban nightlife has developed into a phenomenon . . . and it may well be the most performed work by a living British playwright.' *Daily Telegraph*

Happy Families: 'Demonstrates how at the hands of a skilled playwright, the emotional concentration of family life is always material for energetic drama. John Godber is skilled in many things – writing, directing, making people laugh – but perhaps his greatest talent is for simplicity. There is not a gesture, a line or a lighting change out of place in *Happy Families*, which achieves so much by demanding so little.' *Yorkshire Post*

Shakers: 'Manages accurately to convey the language and style of today's party-goers . . . This is one of those slices of life that everyone can recognise and laugh at.' *Liverpool Daily Post*

John Godber was born in Upton, near Pontefract, in 1956. He trained as a teacher at Bretton Hall College, Wakefield, did an MA in Drama and an MPhil/PhD in Drama at Leeds University. Since 1984 he has been Artistic Director of Hull Truck Theatre Company. His plays include: *Happy Jack, September in the Rain, Bouncers* (winner of seven Los Angeles Critics Circle awards), *Up 'n' Under* (Olivier Comedy of the Year Award, 1984), *Shakers* and *Shakers Restirred* (both with Jane Thornton), *Up 'n' Under 2, Blood, Sweat and Tears, Teechers, Salt of the Earth, On the Piste, Happy Families* (commissioned by British Telecom for the Little Theatre Guild of Great Britain and premiered by 49 amateur companies on the same night in 1991, the biggest ever theatrical opening), *The Office Party, April in Paris, Passion Killers* and *Lucky Sods*. Television and film work includes: *The Ritz, The Continental, My Kingdom for a Horse, Chalkface* (all BBC2), episodes of *Crown Court, Grange Hill* and *Brookside* and screenplays for *On the Piste* and *Up 'n' Under*. He is an honorary lecturer at Bretton Hall College and a DLitt. of Hull University.

by the same author

JOHN GODBER PLAYS: 2*
(Teechers, Happy Jack, September in the Rain,
Salt of the Earth)

April in Paris
Big Trouble in the Little Bedroom
Blood, Sweat and Tears
Dracula (*with Jane Thornton*)
Gym and Tonic
It Started with a Kiss
Lucky Sods & Passion Killers*
Office Party
On the Piste
Perfect Pitch
Seasons in the Sun
Thick as a Brick
Unleashed
Up 'n' Under
Up 'n' Under 2
Weekend Breaks

* published by Methuen

JOHN GODBER

Plays: 1

Bouncers
1990s Remix

Happy Families

Shakers
Restirred
(*with Jane Thornton*)

introduced by the author

Methuen Drama

METHUEN CONTEMPORARY DRAMATISTS

1 3 5 7 9 10 8 6 4 2

This collection first published in the United Kingdom in 2001 by
Methuen Publishing Limited
215 Vauxhall Bridge Road, London SW1V 1EJ

Bouncers was first published in the United Kingdom in 1987 by
Warner/Chappell Plays Ltd
Bouncers (1990s Remix) was first published in 1993 by
Warner/Chappell Plays Ltd
Copyright © 1987, 1993 by John Godber

Happy Families was first published in the United Kingdom in 1992 by
Samuel French Ltd
Copyright © 1992 by John Godber

Shakers was first published in the United Kingdom in 1987 by
Warner/Chappell Plays Ltd
Shakers Restirred was first published in 1993 by
Warner/Chappell Plays Ltd
Copyright © 1987, 1993 by John Godber and Jane Thornton

Collection and introduction copyright © 2001 by John Godber

The right of the author to be identified as the author of these works
has been asserted by him in accordance with the Copyright, Designs
and Patents Act, 1988

Methuen Publishing Limited Reg. No. 3543167

A CIP catalogue record for this book
is available from the British Library

ISBN 0 413 75810 9

Typeset by Deltatype Ltd, Birkenhead
Printed and bound in Great Britain by
Cox & Wyman Ltd, Reading, Berks

Contents

A Chronology
of first performances

Bouncers (Edinburgh Festival; Hull Truck Theatre
   Company, Donmar Warehouse, 1984)   1977
Cry Wolf (Yorkshire Actors Company)   1981
Cramp (Edinburgh Festival; then Bloomsbury, 1987) 1981
EPA (Minsthorpe High School)   1982
Young Hearts Run Free (Bretton Hall)   1983
A Christmas Carol (Hull Truck)   1984
September in the Rain (Hull Truck)   1984
Up 'n' Under 1 (Hull Truck, Edinburgh Festival;
   then Donmar Warehouse)   1984
Shakers (with Jane Thornton. Hull Truck)   1984
Happy Jack (Hull Truck)   1985
Up 'n' Under 2 (Hull Truck)   1985
Cramp (musical. Hull Truck)   1986
Blood, Sweat and Tears (Hull Truck; then Tricycle
   Theatre)   1986
Oliver Twist (Hull Truck)   1987
Teechers (Hull Truck, Edinburgh Festival; Arts
   Theatre, 1988)   1987
Salt of the Earth (Wakefield Centenary; then
   Hull Truck, Edinburgh Festival; then Donmar
   Warehouse)   1988
Office Party (Nottingham Playhouse)   1989
On the Piste (Hull Truck, Derby Playhouse;
   Garrick, 1993)   1990
Everyday Heroes (with Jane Thornton. Community
   play, Bassetlaw)   1991
Bouncers, 1990s Re-mix (Hull Truck)   1991
Shakers Re-stirred (with Jane Thornton. Hull
   Truck)   1991
Happy Families (Little Theatre Guild, West
   Yorkshire Playhouse, 1992)   1991
April in Paris (Hull Truck; Ambassadors, 1994)   1992
Passion Killers (Hull Truck, Derby Playhouse)   1994

Lucky Sods (Hull Truck; then Hampstead Theatre)	1995
Dracula (with Jane Thornton. Hull Truck)	1995
Gym and Tonic (Hull Truck, Derby Playhouse)	1996
Weekend Breaks (Hull Truck, Alhambra, Bradford)	1997
It Started with a Kiss (Hull Truck)	1997
Unleashed (Hull Truck, Edinburgh Festival; Bloomsbury, 1999)	1998
Hooray for Hollywood (Hull Truck)	1998
Perfect Pitch (Stephen Joseph Theatre, Scarborough)	1998
Big Trouble in the Little Bedroom (Hull Truck)	1999
Seasons in the Sun (Hull Truck, West Yorkshire Playhouse)	2000
Thick as a Brick (Hull Truck)	2000

We gratefully acknowledge the help of John Bennett and Liverpool Hope University College in the preparation of this chronology. Further information can be found on www.johngodber.co.uk.

Introduction

Before I try to make some sense of this collection of plays, I have to set the record straight with regard to *Shakers*. The play is often attributed to me, but in truth it was in every way a collaboration between myself and Jane Thornton. Jane is an actress, a writer in her own right and more latterly my wife. Since now I have admitted the rightful owners of these plays I will proceed to explain why they represent a kind of scope in my theatrical work.

It certainly could be said that two of the plays included here, *Bouncers* and *Shakers*, are from a similar school of theatrical thought. Indeed the genesis of the collaboration was an attempt to produce a play for women which had the same sense of excitement, the same visceral energy and calls upon the audience's engaged imagination as its bigger brother *Bouncers*. There were certainly times when *Bouncers* was enjoying huge success that any number of actresses approached us for something similar for women: in a way *Shakers* – however different – was an answer to those kinds of demands.

So if *Bouncers* and *Shakers* share a common theatrical philosophy, what is that philosophy? To answer this question we need to scroll back over the years, to my first engagement with the theatre as an art form. We may even have to investigate some biographical details, which could throw light on why the form of *Bouncers* was chosen, and why the same writer came to write something as different as *Happy Families*, a wholly autobiographical piece.

It has to be said from the start that there was little or no history of theatrical interest in my family. I was born into a mining family, and consequently the notion of my finding employment as a miner was not out of the question. Indeed this became more of a reality when I failed my eleven-plus and was consigned to Upton Secondary Modern School. Upton Secondary Modern was 'secondary and not very modern', as I later wrote in

Happy Families. But on reflection this is rather a glib picture, for as I recall it now, the English teacher in the school encouraged the performance of plays, and at the age of twelve I had already written a short sketch which appeared to make the audience laugh. A year later, I was rescued from the tripartite system by the adoption in West Yorkshire of the comprehensive system, and discovered drama for real during the six years I spent at Minsthorpe High School.

While at Minsthorpe I continually felt I had to justify the interest I found in this new subject. Even though the school was forward-thinking in that every child had to study drama, art and music, I always felt that my fascination with acting was frowned upon by friends and family. Indeed when I eventually opted to train as a drama teacher, my mother wondered long and hard why I didn't want to study to be a history teacher – clearly something which appeared more 'real' to her than 'farting about in plays'.

During the early seventies I trained as a teacher of Drama at Bretton Hall College near Wakefield. It was during this time that a great many of my beliefs and ideas about theatre began to emerge. Indeed the first-ever version of *Bouncers* appeared in 1977 with two un-named Bouncers, Tall and Short, fronting up a disco. The show was taken to the Edinburgh Festival and on the first performance an audience of two made light work of the play. One, a drunk, came on stage and started chatting with us; the second, a critic from the *Scotsman*, left when we started chatting to the drunk and we never saw a review. However on the second night of the play, the actor Brian Glover and a number of his friends from Nottingham Playhouse sought out our less than perfect venue, watched the play, and gave a few words of encouragement. It was enough for me to continue my interest in drama and plays, and even though we didn't attract another single punter for the rest of our week at the Festival, we returned to Wakefield flushed with success.

Several years later when I had left Leeds University's
Workshop Theatre and the MA course there I began
teaching back at my former school, Minsthorpe. I have to
admit that I still felt I had to justify my subject to friends
and colleagues, despite having spent five years in full-time
study and having secured a place to study for a PhD part-
time. This insecurity I attribute to failing my eleven-plus.

Now throughout all this time, it has to be noted that I
had more than a passing interest in sport. I had played
football, table tennis and rugby at school. I had continued
to play rugby at college and university, and had become
involved with body-builders and weight-lifters during my
early twenties. It was a bizarre mix for many, but I took
some comfort from Brecht's relationship with boxers, and
the massive German actor Oscar Homolka. Literature
and Sport could interface and the West Yorkshire
coalfields seemed to be the perfect place. At that time I
used to joke that I was any disruptive kid's nightmare, I
was a seventeen-stone drama teacher with a PhD.

I was so fascinated by plays at this time that I would
read a play each weekend before turning out to play
rugby for Hemsworth Rugby Club. By the early eighties
there wasn't a play in the Penguin series that I hadn't
read; drama was my life!

In 1981, a number of actor friends set up a company,
Yorkshire Actors. They asked me if I would like to re-visit
Bouncers and present it as a four-hander. It was the
opportunity I needed to bring a number of strands
together.

I had become increasingly bored by the conventions of
modern drama. Most of the plays I had read were set in
realistic locations, and therefore fairly limiting in terms of
how they could represent themselves to an audience. In
some respects these plays amounted to nothing more than
'big telly' – true they had good stories and incisive
characterisation, but in terms of their theatrical scope, the
four walls of the box set seemed to limit their vision. Of
course I was not the first to recognise this: Berkoff,

Edward Gordon Craig, Brecht, Artaud and sundry others had all identified this limitation, and had done work to counter the spread of this particular theatrical virus.

And so it was, with all the above in mind, that I set out to re-draw *Bouncers*. I wanted to tell of a nightmarish night in the discos of England from the bouncers' point of view. I had the restrictions of a four-actor budget, something I was very much used to in school productions, and since there was equally no budget for a set, I thought it perhaps best not to have one.

The emphasis would be on the actors/bouncers; they would play all the characters in a roller-coaster of an evening. The play would be funny, but it would also attempt to tell the truth. Like the best of lessons it would be entertaining and thoughtful at one and the same time. The actors/bouncers would play women by the aid of a handbag, they would play the lads on the town, and as well as playing the bouncers they would be standing at the door of the theatre even before the play began. There was nothing much new in this however. Charles Marowitz had done similar things at the Open Space in London with *Fortune and Men's Eyes*, set in a Canadian reformatory.

What was perhaps different was the way in which the actors playing the bouncers admitted the illusion of the theatrical experience. Even before the play gets under way they tell the audience they will 'try to illustrate the sort of things that happen late'. They are almost apologising for the fact that they are only bouncers and not adept in the skills of the theatre. It is of course a false conceit but it creates a tension in the audience, the lines of reality are somewhat blurred, especially after we have seen the bouncers showing members of the public to their seats and taking tickets.

Later, when one actor/bouncer changes character in front of the audience, another actor/bouncer says to the audience 'I thought he was the barber?'. It is still as if the play is trundling along with the actors/bouncers not in control of the illusion, which of course they clearly are.

On other occasions Lucky Eric, the wise old owl of the
bouncers, has a number of speeches. Each speech is
acknowledged as a speech, with no attempt to ask the
audience to buy into the concept of monologue. 'Lucky
Eric's first speech . . . Lucky Eric's fourth and final
speech.' In fact throughout the play the actors play with
the duality of performance. At one moment they are
threatening bouncers and a moment later they are
mincing young girls, but throughout this they are aware of
the game they are playing with the audience.

It is a dangerous game, they do not have the bric-à-brac
of realism to fall back on. They do not have a set or cups
and saucers to rely on, they cannot be contextualised by
'flapping canvas scenery'. They simply have physical
precision, energy, muscular control, and they have the
audience's imagination: they are naked save for their skills
as performers.

This style of presentation which mixes the broadly
popular with the gauche game of theatrical paradox keeps
an audience on its toes. As the play changes genre and
direction from moment to moment, the audience cannot
relax intellectually since they are unsure where the next
moment will come from and what their response will be.
There is a narrative, but it is slight, there are observations,
but they are cartoon, there is social commentary but it is
peppered with outrageous humour. When the whole thing
works there is a pure state of theatrical engagement.

I suppose it was through an attempt to reach a wider
audience that I settled for this particular form. Since the
lack of interest in the theatre I had experienced from
friends and school kids, I wanted to make a piece of
theatre that couldn't be ignored. A piece of theatre where
the audience couldn't switch off momentarily and look at
the set; a piece of theatre that was robust and vigorous,
shocking and humorous. I wanted to create a piece of
theatre that spoke to a generation of clubbers rather than
theatregoers, and spoke to them in a language which they
understood. The pace had to be fast, it had to be slick,

and it had to be funny. It had to be worth going out to
see!

I also wanted to make something that showed actors
working hard, sweating with their efforts. In some ways,
maybe I was craving acceptance from a working-class
audience, who had perhaps been working hard and
sweating all day. In some respects then, I wanted to create
a piece of work that would stand up and justify its place in
a working-man's world! No, I wanted to create a piece of
theatre that would justify its existence in any world!

Of course the subject matter was of prime importance.
In many ways the content informed the form. The
boredom of the men on the door spills over into grotesque
violence and fantasy. The antics of the girls and boys out
for a night on the town hardly need developing to make
them dramatic. The conflict between those wanting a
good time and those stopping a good time from being had
is a basic dramatic premise. In some ways I simply
recorded what I saw every Friday and Saturday night, in
and around Pontefract and Wakefield. Perhaps the skill is
in how the story is told, rather than the story itself.

Certainly when I first thought of *Bouncers*, I could hardly
have imagined the kind of life it would have, or its
influence on other generations. I certainly didn't think of
it as a classic, but then I suppose everyone will be eighteen
at least once in their life and despite ever-changing music
styles, House, Garage, Garbage, Muck, Rubbish, call it
what you will, the central theme of *Bouncers* is universal:
men after beer after women, and the beat goes on.

So it was with the same kind of desire and philosophy
that Jane and I put *Shakers* together. The tone here,
however, is altogether softer. The play was originally
written at a time when old pubs were changing into
cocktail bars almost overnight. It seems that fashion is
changing so frequently that the cocktail bars have been
replaced by theme pubs, which in turn are being re-fitted
as coffee-houses. Essentially, however, the plight of the
waitresses is the same, and it was a deliberate desire to

attempt to draw the characters of the women with more
detail that perhaps results in the pace being more realistic
and much less nightmarish than its model. Nevertheless
Shakers remains as much an exercise for actresses – asking
for precision in role-playing and definition in
characterisation – as *Bouncers* does.

Given the emphasis on the physical, on cartoon
sketches, on speed and an MTV style of theatre, one
would be forgiven for wondering where on earth *Happy
Families* came from. This is a much more lyrical play than
either *Bouncers* or *Shakers*. It is autobiographical,
sentimental, domestic and insular, and yet it is quite
theatrical at the same time. The narrator John speaks
directly to the audience, arranging his/my life in a series
of vignettes. The influences on this style of writing seem to
be a cross-fertilisation between the trilogy of Neil Simon's
rites-of-passage plays and the work of the famous Polish
director Tadeusz Kantor. John takes us through the play
from his eleven-plus failure to his graduation day as a
drama teacher.

It is a memory play, and with memory not all things are
prepared in an orderly fashion. Early parts of the
narrative jump backwards and forwards in time, in the
same way that a conversation might do. When his
grandparents die, they do not leave the action, as they
would do in a wholly realistic drama; they remain on stage
commenting on the action, as they would have done were
they still alive. This is another theatrical conceit, a game
played with the audience and with the cast, and a source
of a good deal of humour. But like *Bouncers* and *Shakers* the
humour is not slapstick, it is felt, human and tinged with
sadness. As I think someone once said of Ben Jonson,
'comedy can exaggerate but it can never lie'. For me,
there has to be pain or there is no comedy, comedy
without release or without counterpoint to this absurd
journey called living is just froth.

Of course *Happy Families* comes much later than the
previous two plays. I think it is fair to say that as I have

got older I have taken more pleasure in the prolonged scene, in a character's development, in the psychology of the drama, in peeling back the layers of the onion. Of course subject matter has a huge influence on how a piece may come together. The form of *Bouncers* is wholly unsuitable for a memory play about my development as a teenager, and perhaps I am less desperate to impress those whom I wanted to impress with *Bouncers*. And yet I still have that ache which reminds me that theatre should be relevant, that it should speak directly and vividly to the audience.

So if there is a theme running between these three plays maybe it is simply a celebration of the diversity of theatre writing. For my own part I appear to swing between the two poles of visceral writing and lyrical writing with each new play I begin. And having written some forty or so theatrical pieces I continually ask myself why I would want to write another one; the answer is simple, to write a better play, in all respects!

John Godber
Hull
July 2000

Bouncers
1990s Remix

Bouncers was first presented by Hull Truck Theatre Company at the Assembly Rooms, Edinburgh, as part of the Edinburgh Festival Fringe on 11 August 1984, transferring to the Donmar Warehouse Theatre, London, in September. The cast was as follows:

Lucky Eric	Peter Geeves
Judd	Richard Ridings
Ralph	Richard May
Les	Andrew Dunn

Directed by John Godber

This version of *Bouncers* first performed in 1991, directed by John Godber for Hull Truck, with the following cast:

Lucky Eric	Charlie Dickinson
Judd	Adrian Hood
Ralph	Ian Rogerson
Les	Mick Callaghan

Act One

*Eric *and the bouncers have been parading the auditorium. As
the music plays they enter the stage. An open space. **Les**, **Judd**
and** Ralph** stand upstage. **Eric** addresses the audience. There
is a sense of menace throughout.

Eric Ladies and gentlemen, we present the Bouncers
Remix.

Judd/Ralph/Les Bouncers! (*Elongating the 'S'.*)

Eric
We welcome you to a vision
Of the nineties urban night-life
To stag nights and hen-do's
To drunken crying girls and gallons of booze.

Judd/Ralph/Les (*singing*)
Celebration time, come on!

Eric
It's always frustrating
For the oldest swingers in town
Yes all human life is inevitably here
In a midnight circus
And I must make it clear
That the beer is pricey, the music pulsating
The atmosphere is intoxicating
We four will try to illustrate
The sort of things that happen late
At night in every town
When the pubs are shut
And the beer's been downed . . .

Now down at the disco is the place to be
The lights are so bright
Like a colour TV
The music is loud
And the beer flows free

It's a disco placc for you and me
Now on the door, you pay your money
The place is packed, the place is funny
Look at the girls . . .

All   Mmmmmmmm . . .

Eric
Smell their honey
Come to the place
Where the beat pulsates
In the heat of the night
The walls gyrate
In the bowels of hell
The scent is strong
There's sex in the air
And the hunt is on
And the children of England
Sing their song

All (*slowly*)
Here we go, here we go, here we go . . .

A pause.

Les/Judd
Well you finish work

Ralph/Eric
Well it's Friday night

Les/Judd
So you've got your pay . . .

Ralph/Eric
And you feel alright

All
Pump up the bitter
Pump up the bitter
Pump up the bitter
Down eight pints
You don't ca-care care

You don't ca-care care
You don't ca-care care
'Cos it's Friday night

Eric
I said hip-hippy

Judd
Gip-gippy

All
Hip gip hop bop
Drink that slop and don't you stop

Eric
Get down get up get in get out

Judd/Eric
Get down get up get in get out

Les/Judd/Eric
Get down get up get in get out

All
Get down get up get in get out

Eric
The bouncers are mean
In their black and white
The fellas are pissed
But their fists are tight
But the chicks are loose

All (*as women*)
'Cos it's Friday niiiight . . .

Eric
We got soul

All
Rap

Eric
We got soul

All
  House rap

Eric
  We play a lot of other stuff

Judd
  That sounds like crap

All (*building*)
  Get down get up
  Get in get out
  Get down get up
  Get in get out
  Get down get up
  Get in get out

Eric
  If you come down here
  Wearing jeans

Judd
  You can't get in

All
  Know what he means?
  Gotta have a tie, gotta have a suit
  Gotta look cute or you'll get the boot
  Gotta have a tie, gotta have a suit
  Gotta look cute or you'll get the boot

They are stage centre. A spotlight picks them out.

Les   You're listening to Radio Bollocks. 'Hello Steve, it's Gervaise here, keep your tongue out and I'll call you right back.'

All   Ten fifty-three. Ten eighty-nine. Radio One FM.

Ralph (*as Bowie*)   Tell me what the time is, tell me what the temperature is.

Les   Yes that was the Bouncers, strange name for a group that.

Ralph Yes yes yesh boy yesh boy get a pen . . . get
a pen . . .

Judd Fillet o' fish, fillet o' fish, give me a fish to
fillet.

Les Yes. That record is going down very well in the
discos so I shall certainly be playing it tonight at my
gig in Littlehampton.

Ralph Yes indeed.

All Yes we do.

Judd Let's have that off.

*Suddenly the scene changes and the bouncers become female
customers in a ladies' hairdresser.* **Ralph** *sits under a hairdryer,
reading a magazine.* **Eric** *(Maureen) is having his hair washed
by* **Judd** *(Cheryl).* **Les** *is offstage.*

Judd That Steve Wright gets up my ring . . . and
he's so popular because people keep ringing him up.
Do you listen to it, Maureen?

Eric No, Cheryl love. It gets on my bloody nerves. I
like that Bruno Brooks and Gaz-za-za Davies.

Judd This new Alberto Balsam should do wonders
for your hair, Maureen.

Eric Do you think so?

Judd Oh yeah.

Eric I want to look nice for tonight.

Judd Going anywhere special?

Eric It's Rosie's twenty-first. It should be a good do.

Judd I hope it is, love.

Eric You know her. She comes in here. She works at
our place. Four of us are going down to Mr Cinders.

Judd Oh, I've heard some good reports about that
place.

Eric Yes. It's alright.

All Yes. It's alright.

Eric It's the best place round here.

Judd It's all plush, isn't it?

Eric Yeah. You've got to get there early to get in. It gets packed out. Like the Black Hole of bloody Calcutta.

Les *enters the hairdresser's, out of breath. He has become Rosie.*

Les Hiya.

All Hiya.

Les Chuffin' hell. Talk about being rushed off your feet. Look at the time and I've only just finished.

Eric What've you been up to, Rosie?

Les An order came in at ten to four.

Eric Chuffin' cheek.

Les Friday and all. And my bleeding birthday.

All Cheeky getts.

Les Can you fit me in, Cheryl?

Judd I can't, I'm afraid, love. I'm chock-a-block till seven.

Ralph I told her to book.

Judd I'm going out myself . . . Dagonara Casino.

Eric Gambling?

Judd Well . . .

All Bloody 'ell.

Les I'll just have to be late, that's all. I'll nip over to

Barbara's. She might be able to fit me in. I'll see you down here later, Maureen.

Eric Alright, luv.

Les Tara, luvs.

All Tara.

Les (*to audience*) Tara everyone.

Eric She's a dizzy sod, that Rosie.

Ralph (*getting uncomfortable under the hairdryer*) How much longer, Cheryl?

Judd Bloody hell. She's on fire!

Eric Cheryl.

Judd Bloody hell. I wish you'd get your hair cut.

Eric I've got a new sort of skirt thing. It's nice, a bit tight, but so what? Ski pants as well.

Judd C&A?

Eric No.

Judd Top Shop?

Eric No chance. Got it from Chelsea Girl.

Judd/Ralph Chelsea Girl.

Judd Oh yeah. They're lovely. I've got one in a sort of maroon.

Eric/Ralph Maroon.

Judd I got them in the sale.

Eric How much were they?

All Barbers!

Although the scene remains exactly the same we are now in a barber's. **Judd** *is a brusque barber.* **Eric** *is in the chair.* **Ralph** *reads a dirty magazine.*

Judd   Come and get your hair cut if you dare.

Ralph   Jesus Christ! Where is he?

Eric   I can't see him.

Judd   I'm over here, lads. Right. Who wants what? You young lads want a proper haircut. Well, for three fifty you can have the Vinnie Jones look. Very popular with the thugs. Or for three fifty you can have the Elephant Man cut.

Eric   What's the Elephant Man cut?

Judd   It makes one side of your head look bigger than the other.

Ralph   Funny barber.

Judd   You said it.

Ralph   I wouldn't let him near me.

Eric   Why?

Ralph   Look at his own hair.

Judd (*ignoring them*)   Or you can have the Tony Curtis haircut look.

Eric   Hey, what's the Tony Curtis haircut look?

Judd   All off. Totally bald. Egghead cut.

Eric   Tony Curtis doesn't have his hair cut like that . . .

Judd   He does if he comes in here. Funny, eh? Funny, lads, eh?

Eric   Just cut it, will yer and cut the gags.

Eric *gets in the chair and* **Judd** *begins to cut his hair.*

Judd   Going somewhere, are we?

Eric   Disco.

Judd How old are you?

Ralph (*looking at a magazine*) Juddy hell! Look at the body on that.

Eric I'm nineteen.

Judd Got a woman?

Ralph I hope that she's down there tonight.

Eric I might have at two o'clock.

Judd Make sure that you don't get an ugly one.

Ralph There's only ugly ones left at two o'clock.

Eric Bollocks, Jerry.

Judd Watch the language, you.

Ralph What are you doing to his hair? He can't go out like that . . . hey you can keep away from me, you bleeding maniac.

Judd Anything on?

Eric No thanks.

Judd Anything for the weekend?

Ralph Yeah, I'll have a gross.

Eric What time are we starting?

Ralph Time they do open.

Les *enters.*

Les I'm here, you dreamers.

All Kev.

Eric Kev, ready for the big night.

Les Ready as I'll ever be.

Ralph Hey. I am dying for it. I've starved myself all week.

Eric   He's a dirty sod.

Les   Seven o'clock in the Taverners, right?

Eric/Ralph   Right.

Les   Alright.

Eric/Ralph   Alright.

Les   Where's Terry?

Judd   I'm here.

Judd *switches from playing the barber to playing Terry. The scene changes to a street corner where they all wait for Terry.*

All   I thought he was the barber.

Judd   Just finished a mindless day of wood stackin', talking about the races at Chepstow, the dogs at White City and the chances of England winning the World Cup . . .

All (*chanting*)   Engla-and.

Judd   . . . ready for the night-time. Mindless girl-watching and a chance perhaps of the old sniff of perfume and feel of inside thigh; milky-white thighs and bloodshot eyes. It's no surprise that I'm dying for it.

All   See you down there at seven.

All   Terry–Jerry–Kev–Baz –

Judd   Be young –

Eric   Be foolish –

Les   But be happy –

All   Be da da da da da da da da . . .

Ralph   And be careful not to catch it!

All   Bollocks!

The actors now become the lads getting ready for the big night out.

Eric Baz, that is it. Friday night, fit for a fight. Get down there. Have a skinful. Might have a Chinese, or a chicken-in-the-basket. Maybe a hot-dog. Might risk it. Got my dole money saved up. Try and pull some skirt. Give her a pup.

Ralph I'm looking cool. I'm looking great. Wish I didn't have that spot. (*He squeezes an imaginary spot.*) Gotcha! Blackheads. Slap some Clearasil on my face. Not bad, Jerry. Not bad at all, mate.

Eric Hope I don't get stabbed again.

Judd Time is it?

Les Jesus Christ ...

Ralph Ten to seven.

Les Gonna be late.

Ralph Time for another quick check.

They all stand in a row and check the various parts of their bodies.

Eric Hair?

All Check.

Judd Tie?

All Check.

Eric Aftershave? Jason Donovan uses this.

All (*sing*)
  Sealed With a Kiss ... Check.

Eric Talc on genitals?

All Check.

Eric Clean underpants?

Ralph Well . . .

Les They'll do.

Eric Money?

All Double check.

Les Condoms?

All Checkaroonie.

Judd Breath?

They all breathe out and try and smell their own breath.

All Ugh! Beer should drown that.

Judd Right. That's it then. We're ready. Catch the bus at the end of our street.

Ralph Ding ding.

Les Fares please.

Eric Bollocks.

Judd Get downtown to start the pub crawl. When we get there it's packed already. I see me mates. Baz, Jerry an' Kev an' me into the Taverners.

During the following sequence the lads attempt to get served. Their actions should convey the bustling, pushy atmosphere of a pub.

Judd Four pints, please!

All (*as they down the first pint of the evening*)   ONE!

Les 'Course I'm eighteen.

Eric Get some crisps.

Judd Four bags of beef.

Ralph Look at tits on that.

All (*to audience*)   Social comment.

Judd   Four pints, pal.

All   TWO!

Ralph   Hey, who's pushing?

Eric   Are you being served?

Les   Hey up, bastard.

Ralph   Four more pints, pal.

All   THREE!

Judd   Got any pork scratchings?

Eric   Hey, watch me shirt.

Ralph   Look who's pushing?

Les   Packed in't it?

Judd   Lct me get to them bogs.

Eric   Excuse me.

Ralph   Four pints

All   FOUR!

Judd   And a whisky, love, please.

All   FIVE!

Eric   Excuse me, love.

Les   I gave you a fiver.

Judd   Fat gett.

Ralph   Four pints, four bags of beef, four bags of salted peanuts and four whisky chasers.

All (*thumbs*)   Yeah! SIX! SEVEN!

Judd   Have you got any cashews?

Eric   Hey twat, I've been stood here a month.

Les   Can we have some service down here?

Ralph   I'm next, love.

Eric   Shut your mouth, skullhead.

Judd   I'm being served, love, thanks.

*The four lads recoil as they see beer spill all over **Eric**'s (Baz's) trousers.*

Eric   Ooooooh! Look at that. Somebody's spilt beer all over my suit.

Judd   Daft gett.

Eric   It's brand new.

Les   It'll dry.

Judd   How many have we had?

Ralph   Ten.

Judd   Time for another.

Eric   I've only had nine.

Ralph   Are we off?

Eric   D'you think we'll get in?

Judd   Should do.

Les   Hope there's no trouble.

Eric   There's four of us.

All   Yeah.

Ralph   Come on. Let's get down there, pick something up.

All   Right.

Eric   Hang on.

Les   What?

Eric   Piss call.

All   Oh yeah.

They all turn their backs as if peeing and then turn back to face the audience.

Judd We'd better split up.

Les Why?

Judd The bouncers.

Eric Don't let you in. In groups.

Ralph OK. Me and Kev. Right.

Judd Yeah. And me and . . . (*Realising who he's paired off with.*) Oh bollocks!

Just as they are about to move away they all freeze. Pause. They once more become the girls we saw earlier in the hairdresser sequence. **Eric** *(Maureen),* **Les** *(Rosie),* **Judd** *(Elaine), and* **Ralph** *(Suzy) all stand together in a circle having a laugh and a drink in a pub. They are all dressed up in their brand new clothes ready for the night out. This should be communicated to the audience through their actions. They introduce themselves one by one.*

Eric Maureen. Massive but nice. Fat but cuddly. Not a bag, but likes a drink and a laugh. A bit busty. (*Silly laugh.*)

Les Rosie. Birthday today. Tall and slim, hair all permed. I had it done at Barbara's.

Eric It's nice. It really suits you.

Les Thank you.

Eric Cow.

Les I've had a drink. I feel a bit tiddly. Hey, it will end in tears. Hello luv.

Eric Hello.

Les Have you lost a bit of weight?

Judd Plain Elaine.

Eric/Les   It's a shame.

Judd   Left school at sixteen with one GCSE in metalwork. I'm on the dole.

Eric/Les   It's such a shame.

Judd   Enjoys a good night out but doesn't expect to get picked up though. Handy in a fight . . . come here ya bastard. Hiya

Eric/Les   Hiya.

Ralph   Rose, Maureen, Elaine . . . Hiya.

All   Hiya Suzy.

Ralph   Sexy . . . I've got stockings on under my dress. Do you wanna look? You cheeky getts! Go on then. Anybody's for half a lager. Goes under the sunbed . . . brown all over. I bet you would fancy it, big boy. Ooh, he's nice that one. Is that your head or has your neck thrown up?

Les   I'll say he is. Yeah. Right. Who wants what?

Judd   I'll have a pint of Guinness . . . no, only a joke. I'll have a brandy and lime.

Eric   Well. I'll have a lager and black because if I have any more I'll be on my back.

Les   As usual.

Eric   You cheeky sod.

Les   Sorry.

Ralph   I'll have a Piña Colada.

Eric   Christ. Listen to her.

Ralph   Well I'm eighteen.

Les   She doesn't bloody care. I feel a bit sick.

Eric   You'll be alright when we get down there.

Les   Are we getting the bus?

Ralph   Well, I'm not walking it in these shoes.

All   They're lovely.

Ralph   I know.

Judd   I'm gonna put a record on.

All   Ya da da da da da da ya da da da da.

Judd *walks up to an imaginary juke-box, represented by* **Eric**. **Les** *and* **Ralph** *join* **Judd** *around the juke-box.*

Ralph   Put that on 3A. I like that.

Judd   No. It's crap.

Les   I think you should put Wham on.

Judd   I'm putting on a funky disco record.

Ralph   I'm afraid you are not, because I like this one here by Bros. (*Repeats as if the record is sticking.*)

All   When will I be famous?

Sudden blackout and freeze. The actors walk to the side of the stage. A dark and foreboding sound filters out from the speakers. The pace has been fast and hectic up until this point, but now the stage is quite still. We are outside the club. Eerie, disturbing music plays as we move into a mime sequence during which the bouncers come to life. During this sequence each actor should create and display a kind of larger-than-life character for each bouncer. It is at this point that the individual characteristics of each bouncer are established. Ordinary mannerisms and gestures are grotesquely exaggerated as, one by one, the bouncers step forward to introduce themselves through mime. **Judd***, for example, walks slowly and cautiously to the centre of the stage, looks around, takes a hand exerciser out of his pocket and begins to do a series of exercises. He does so to the point of exhaustion, his face grimacing as the seeping pain of lactic acid invades his forearm muscles. He puts away the exerciser and has a moment's silence to himself. He takes a comb out of his pocket and begins* *to carefully comb his hair. When he has completed this highly meticulous activity, he puts the comb away and enjoys another moment's contemplation. He spits on the floor, rubs the spit into the ground with his foot and then cracks his knuckles. All these actions are executed with the greatest attention to detail and are outrageously heightened as indicated above. Once* **Judd** *has finished his sequence,* **Ralph** *moves centre stage and repeats the ritual. When he has finished, he stands by* **Judd**. **Les** *joins them, once more enacting the ritual. Finally they speak. Each word is delivered with much more emphasis than would appear necessary as they acknowledge each other.*

Les   Judd?

Judd   Les.

Ralph   Les?

Les   Ralph.

Ralph   Judd?

Judd   Ralph.

Lucky **Eric** *joins the group.*

Eric   Ralph?

Ralph   Lucky Eric.

Judd   Eric?

Eric   Judd, Les.

Les   Lucky Eric. Alright?

Eric   Yeah. Why?

Les   Cold innit?

Ralph   Yeh. Bitter.

Judd   Any trouble last night?

Les   Usual. Couple of punks got glassed.

Judd   Nothing special then?

Ralph No.

Les I wanted to have 'em, but Eric said no.

Eric You're too violent, Les. You can't control yourself.

Les You don't have any fun, Eric. That's your trouble. Gerrin' past it.

Eric (*totally manic*) Don't you ever say that I am getting past it! Ever! (*Moves to* **Les**.)

Judd Many in?

Ralph Packed. Early rush, then it'll tail off.

Eric That's Fridays for you.

Judd I got a basket meal for nothing yesterday.

Eric When?

Judd Yesterday.

Les Who gave it to you?

Judd That girl.

Eric Oh yeah?

Ralph Nice one she is, nice tea-bag.

Judd Not bad.

Eric Yeah, alright in the dark.

Ralph A bit fat around the buttocks if you ask me.

Eric Sommat to grab innit?

Judd Chicken it was. Tender.

Les And chips?

Judd No chips. Fattening!

Eric Short legs.

Ralph Yeah right.

Eric Optical illusion, that is.

Judd What? That chips are fattening?

Ralph How come?

Eric Makes her arse look bigger.

Les Nearer to the ground.

Ralph Good centre of gravity, chickens.

Eric How's the judo?

Ralph Not bad thanks.

Eric Still training?

Ralph Yeah, twice a week. And you?

Judd Couldn't train hamsters.

Eric I trained you though, didn't I?

Judd Didn't train the wife too well though, did you rubber gob?

Eric Leave my wife out of it you.

Judd I hear she's putting it about a bit.

Eric Don't believe all you hear Judd, your head'll blow up.

Judd I know a bloke who says he's had her.

Les Leave it Judd.

Eric I could have you any time.

Judd The King is dead, Eric.

Eric Every day I go powerlifting, get the hate out of my body, squeeze the pain out of my chest. I bench-pressed three hundred and fifty-four pounds yesterday.

Judd Who?

Eric Me.

Les   When?

Eric   Yesterday.

Les   Get pillocked.

Eric   No pillock Doubting Thomas, no pillock.

Judd   You couldn't press a button.

Eric   Could have done two reps.

Judd   Three hundred and fifty-four pounds, that's er ... fifteen pounds in a stone? Eight stones in a kilo?

Ralph   That's heavy, Judd.

Eric   What can you bench Judd?

Judd   Something.

Eric   Still wrestling?

Judd   No.

Les   Still on the dole aren't you?

Judd   No.

Ralph   Doing a bit of nicking?

Judd   No. Well a bit.

Eric   It's a bit quiet out here tonight, isn't it ... too quiet.

Ralph   It'll soon liven up when the pubs turn out. They'll all be streaming down here, like sheep.

All (*chanting*)   Here we go, here we go, here we go. (*As if downing another pint.*) FOURTEEN!

Ralph   Bastards!

Eric   What time is it?

Judd   Well, the big hand is on nine ...

Les   Early doors yet. No need to start gerrin'

aggressive.

Ralph   Yes, they'll all be coming down here, looking for a woman.

Les   Yeah, a big buxom woman.

Judd   Or a small petite woman.

Eric   Or a bloke.

Judd   Yes, there's usually one or two of them about and all.

Eric   Is there?

Les   They're alright you know really.

Ralph   No, they are not alright you know really.

Les   They are ... they are the same as us. They've got the same feelings, the same sex drives.

Eric   Have they, Leslie?

Les   Yes they have, 'cos one of my best mates ...

Ralph   Hold on a minute, Les.

Eric   What are you on about Les?

Les   Now listen. I was just about to say ...

Ralph   Yes ...

Les   That one of my best mates ...

Ralph   Yes ...

Les   Once knew a fella who once and only once, worked in a club for gay people.

Ralph   Tell us another one.

Eric   You can't be too careful these days, Les.

Ralph   Each to their own. That's it. Each to their bloody own. You have just got to let people get on with what they want ... that is my philosophy for life.

Eric Fair enough Ralph. Fair enough. I like to hear a man express his philosophy. Fair enough. (*Pause.*) You can borrow my handbag any night, sweetie.

Ralph Steady on.

Eric Yeah?

Ralph Steady on.

Eric Or what?

Ralph Are we trying to start something, Eric?

Eric Could be.

Ralph Are we trying to encourage a conflict situation?

Eric Might be, Mr Inner Calm.

Ralph *takes up a strong stance and invites* **Eric** *to hit him.*

Ralph Come on then . . . there . . . now . . .

Eric *makes a move as if to hit him, but stops. It is a hoax.* **Eric** *stands and laughs at* **Ralph**. *The other bouncers see the latent danger but as this is a regular occurrence, they are not unduly disturbed.*

Ralph Powerlifters. I've shit 'em.

Eric Judo. Puffballs.

They back off. There is a moment's quiet.

Judd Eric, Eric . . . Remember that Rugby Union trip that came down.

Les Zulu warriors?

Ralph None of that tonight, I hope.

Judd Caused chaos.

Eric Bloody idiots.

Les College boys.

All (*sing*)
  She's a rag shag-a-bag, she's an automatic whore.

Judd   Chuff heads.

Ralph   College, my arse.

Les   They came down here doing their college antics, hitting each other over the head with beer trays, dropping their trousers every five minutes.

Judd   Like I said, one or two of them about.

Ralph   Animals.

Judd   They have these special nights, you know. Rugby clubs. Sex and all that; live.

Les   Yeah?

Judd   I thought of joining.

Eric   I was just thinking.

Judd   What with?

Eric   My brain, Judd, up here. Where you keep budgie food and dubbin. I've got a brain.

Judd   You ought to be on *Mastermind*, Eric, if you've got a brain. Fancy having a brain and doing this job. At this rate you're going to end up on *Krypton Factor* or sommat.

Eric   And at this rate you're going to end up on a life support, Judd.

Les   Leave it out, Eric.

Ralph   You're very tetchy, Eric.

Eric   Oh yeah?

Ralph   Yes. You're very very tetchy.

Les   What were you thinking about, Eric, with this brain that you've got?

Eric   I was just thinking: women.

Les   Oh yeah, and what about them?

Eric   They're weird!

Les   They're not as weird as having a beard up your arse.

Ralph   What on earth are you trying to say, Eric?

Eric   Different attractions. Strange.

Judd   What's strange about women?

Eric   They laugh at you when you're naked.

All   Oh yeah.

Ralph   I was just thinking as well. I mean, where is everybody? I'm freezing to bloody death out here. Why's that?

Judd   Because it's cold.

Ralph   Because nobody's turned up yet, so let me get me hands on somebody, warm them up a bit.

Judd   They'll all be gerrin' some beer down their bloody necks, stood about in plush pubs, slopping beer down 'em. Either that or they're watching the bloody telly, come down here about half eleven, tight-fisted sods.

Les   It's still early.

Ralph   I'm going inside in a minute.

Eric *has been gazing into the night.*

Eric   Look at them lights, look at all those lights.

Judd   *The City by Night,* by Lucky Eric, 'an artist's impression'.

Les   Piss-artist.

Eric   Them lights are like people, just like people's lives.

Les   What's he on about?

Eric   Them flats, people live in them flats.

Judd   He's a bloody genius, you know.

Eric   Couples, huddled together in one or two rooms.

Ralph   Mom, mom, the rent man's here.

Les   Show him to the bedroom love.

Eric   Carrying out relationships.

Judd   Aye aye, here we go. Getting round to sex.

All   NO NO NO . . . YES!

Eric   In them flats, somebody'll be having a shag right now.

Pause, while the idea sinks in.

Les   Lucky bastards . . .

Eric   All over the world people will be dying, and conceiving children and growing vegetables and shagging.

Les   Lucky bastards.

Ralph   Don't let it get to you, Eric.

Les   Don't get depressed.

Eric   And we're stood here out in the cold like four daft pricks.

Les/Ralph/Judd (*shouting*)   Lucky Eric's first speech!

The three bouncers fade into the background as the lights dim and a spotlight comes up on **Eric**. *He delivers his speech with total sincerity.*

Eric   The girls are young; some look younger than the others. It worries me. It does. I'm not thick. You

think that we're thick. We're not. I'm not. Got to be
eighteen. I turn a blind eye. We live by rules but we
all turn blind eyes. I don't know whether or not it's a
good thing . . . still at school half of them; they come
down here Friday, Saturday, saving up all week the
money they've earned working part-time in the
supermarket. What else is there? With their made-up
faces, floating about on a cloud of Esté Lauder,
wearing Impulse and footless tights, or flashing wrinkle-
free flesh, of schoolgirl knicker dreams, flesh of
sunburnt leg; hairless leg, shapely, untouched-by-
human-hand leg. I sweat a lot. Wouldn't you? Two
drinks and they're going; legs opening to any particular
denizen of the night with car-keys and Aramis-splashed
face, maybe even Old Spice; drunken, free, giddy, silly
girls, wanting to be women, done too soon. Vulnerable,
cruel world the morning after, or the month after
when the curse hasn't taken its spell! I wanna touch
them, squeeze them, keep them safe. Smell like
Pomander, a lingering smell. Pure and dirty, innocent
and vulgar; it all withers, washes away. Eighteen going
on thirty-five, because they think they've got to,
because they're forced to . . . I dunno.

*Lights come up and the other bouncers take up their positions and
start to talk once more — all as if the speech had never occurred.*

Judd Ever have any strange sex, Leslie?

Les No. Never.

Ralph I have. I've had some of that.

Les Yeah? What was it like?

Ralph Strange.

Eric I nearly had chinky once.

Judd Oh yeah. Army, was it?

All Shun . . .

Ralph   In Malaya, was it?

They all make Malaya noises.

Eric   No . . . Fish-and-chip shop down Blenheim
Terrace. Nice woman; didn't understand a word she
said though.

Les   That the language of love, Eric?

Judd   Number 34 with rice, eh?

Ralph   Sixty-nine, knowing Lucky Eric.

They all laugh manically.

Eric   Couldn't go through with it.

Judd   Why?

Eric   Married.

Les   He's crazy.

Judd   I'm in the mood tonight.

Ralph   Tell us something new.

Judd   I could shag a rat.

Ralph   The power of the spoken word.

Lights change, music booms. We are in the disco. **Ralph** *is the
DJ. He speaks nonsense down the microphone. We only catch a
few words. Then he begins the following speech in a spotlight.*

Ralph   Hope that you're all having a greeeaaat time
down here at Mr Cinders. Remember that on
Tuesday, yes that's Tuesday of next week, we'll be
having a video special. Do do come along and enjoy
that extravaganza. I shall be giving away a few bottles
of champagne very shortly for a number of people who
are celebrating their twenty-first today; key of the door
and, let's hope, key of another special place. Are there
any nymphomaniacs down here this evening? Yes,
there are. Well, I'll be playing something for you very

soon, and it will not be a record. OK, OK, let's just stop the music for a moment and put up your hand, yes put up your hand if you are a virgin. I don't believe it, ladies and gentleman, there are no virgins down here this evening. Looks like it's going to be a night to remember. This is Shalamar . . .

The music plays loudly. The four actors now become Elaine, Rosie, Suzy and Maureen. They pick up their handbags and walk with great dignity into the middle of the dance floor. They then all place their handbags in a pile on the floor and begin to dance around the bags to the music.

All (*with the song*)
  'Gonna Make This a Night to Remember'.

Eric   Maureen – short but nice, fat but sickly.

Les   Rosie – feels a bit tiddly.

Judd   Elaine – sweating like a racehorse, wants to sit down.

Ralph   Suzy – sexy and flashing it about a bit.

Judd   Christ, I'm sweating.

Les   Ya what?

Judd   I'm dripping.

Ralph   I am.

Eric   I feel sick . . .

Ralph   You what?

Eric   I feel sick.

Les   It's too warm.

Judd   Ya what Rosie?

Les   I feel dizzy.

Judd/Ralph   Happy birthday.

Les   Shut up.

Eric   I think I'm gonna spew.

Judd   Oh isn't she pathetic?

Eric   Let me get to the toilet.

Les   What's she had?

Ralph   Five barley wines.

Eric   Hang on a minute. I feel alright now, it was just indigestion.

Judd (*to the audience*)   And then, as if by magic, the drunken tears, and Rosie discovers twenty-firsts are not all fun . . .

Eric   Her boyfriend Patrick is seen kissing another . . .

Ralph   With several large shorts imbibed, the tears and mascara begin to run.

Les   He's left me for another, over in a dark corner snogging, and French kissing, tongue job to say the least. I feel myself get all angry and upset inside but I've already had enough drinks to fill a bath. The hate turns inside to self-pity and the tears begin to flow and with it the mascara. And soon my face looks like a miner's back in the showers, rivulets of black Max Factor. And then the friends . . .

All   That's us.

Les   . . . begin to comfort me and offer me advice on how and what to do.

Judd   Burn her face off.

Les   Oh don't be daft, Elaine.

Eric   Castrate the philanderer.

Ralph   Get your LPs back.

Les   Then the plague begins to spread, the tears

begin to flow and all advice becomes sobbing woe.
Look at him sitting there as cool as a cucumber. I've
been going out with him for two days . . . it's pathetic.

All   Pathetic, pathetic, pathetic . . .

Loud music comes up.

Ralph   I love this. I've gorra dance.

Eric   Ooooooooh, it goes right through me.

Ralph   It goes right through me an' all.

Les   What hasn't?

Ralph   I heard that, Rosie.

Les   I'm sorry, Sue.

Ralph   You are not coming to Benidorm.

All   (*with song*)
    Ooh wee . . .

Lights change and we are suddenly outside the club once more.
Eric *and* **Judd** *are the two bouncers, patrolling the doors.*
Ralph *and* **Les** *play a variety of characters trying to enter the*
club.

Eric   Seems to be going quite steady Judd.

Judd   Twenty-nine stones.

Eric   What?

Judd   Twenty-nine stones.

Eric   What is?

Judd   Three hundred and fifty-four pounds. It's heavy
that is Eric, it's twenty-nine stones.

Eric   Right.

Judd   I could bench that.

Eric   Don't start.

Judd   I could beat you any day. I'll have you now.

Eric   Don't.

Judd   I've shit bigger turds than you.

Eric   Leave it.

Judd   Arm wrestle.

Eric   No.

Judd   You're soft.

Eric   Leave it Judd, just leave it.

Judd   The King is dead Eric.

Enter Wak and Wak downstage.

Ralph   Wak.

Les   And Wak, all dressed up very smart.

Ralph   But we look a bit rough.

Both   Hey come ed come ed.

Eric   Evening fellas.

Both   Evening.

Judd   Where are you from?

Les   About.

Judd   Oh yeah?

Eric   Not from round about here though are you?

Ralph   Not from round about here no.

Eric   Oh.

Les   Is there a problem like?

Judd   No, no problem.

Les   Great, we're in, come on.

Eric   Are you out sort of celebrating like?

Ralph   Yeah, you could say that.

Les   Yeah, we're celebrating, yeah.

Eric   What, a stag night is it, lads?

Les   Yeah that's right, a stag night.

Judd   Sorry lads, can't let you in.

Ralph   Why?

Eric   No stag parties allowed in.

Les   You what?

Eric   You heard.

Ralph   Jesus Christ.

Judd   Sorry fellas, but rules is rules.

Ralph/Les   Please.

Eric   Go away.

Ralph/Les   Come ed, come ed, come ed.

Eric   Soft bastards.

Judd   Always works.

Eric   Stag nights; it's always a good laugh.

Judd   No wonder they're losing custom in here.

Ralph *and* **Les** *enter again, this time as punks. They spread their hands above their heads to create spiky hair, spit, spew, pogo, etc.*

Judd   Where are you punks going?

Les   In the discothèque, man.

Eric   Not dressed like that you're not. Go home and change your tutu.

Ralph   Hey man don't mess with my tutu.

Eric   Don't call me man . . . forkhead.

Ralph   Come on man, we're not going to cause any trouble in there. (*He spits.*)

Judd   I know you're not 'cos I'm not going to let you in. (*He spits on* **Ralph**.)

Ralph   Hey did you see that?

Les   Yes I did, and I think it was a very good shot ... come on, let's go and have a pint of piss in the cesspit ...

Ralph   Hey Ruffage.

Les   Yes Ashley.

Ralph   Do you know what they are...? They are fascist pigs ... they've spoilt the whole evening and I am shortly intending to write a song about the experience.

Les   Go on then.

Ralph   Fascist pigs.

Les   Fascist pigs.

Ralph (*singing*)
   Oh you fascist pigs ...

Les (*singing*)
   Oh you fascist pigs ...

Ralph   What do you think of that then?

Les   They're lovely lyrics.

Les *and* **Ralph** *pogo off upstage. The actors suddenly change position so that* **Eric** *and* **Judd** *become the lads, Terry and Baz, and* **Ralph** *and* **Les** *become bouncers once more.*

Eric/Judd (*chanting*)   Here we go, here we go, here we go ...

Eric   Watch these two, Terry.

Judd   Why's that, Baz?

Eric   Might be a bit awkward.

Ralph   Evening, lads.

Eric   Evening.

Les   Are you members?

Judd   You what?

Ralph   Members only tonight, lads, sorry.

Judd   It wasn't members only last night.

Eric   Or last Friday. Play the game, fellas.

Ralph   Only pillocking, lads. In you come. Thirty-eight quid each.

Judd   You what? Hear that, Baz?

Eric   It's only thirty bob.

Les   Let them in, Ralph.

Ralph   You're in. Urine?

Eric *and* **Judd** *enter the club, and walk upstage.*

Ralph   Why did you let them in?

Les   I'm going to do that fat one.

Ralph   You're weird, Les.

Les   Oh yeah.

Ralph   With the greatest respect you're very weird.

Les   I know.

They all now become the lads.

Eric   Baz –

Judd   Terry –

Ralph   Jerry –

Les   Kev –

They all take another imaginary pint and slop it down.

All   SIXTEEN! And a vindaloo!

Les   In the toilets

Eric   Lav

Ralph   Bog

Judd   Shit house!

Standing upstage centre, they are in the club toilets. Each of them passes wind and there is a delight of visual scatological jokes. Finally, they are ready to urinate. **Les** *narrates, conveying the atmosphere while the others act out the situation.*

Les   At about twelve o'clock, the toilets are the hell-hole of the disco. Keeping your feet on the slippery tiled floor is a feat in itself. Many an aff-air has been ruined by loose footing; one quick slip and you're up to your hip in urine.

One of the actors slips and drowns.

When you actually reach the urinals, your Hush Puppies are soaking, seeping through to your socks. In the urinals, there is by this time a liberal smattering of tab ends, and the odd soupçon of sick. In the sink there's probably a Durex packet, with the condoms still inside, some forgetful stud having left them. The smell is nauseous; you stand holding your breath trying to pee, reading the wall, trying your best not to catch anyone's eye.

Eric (*reading*)   You don't come here to mess about to have a piss ... oh, charming ...

Judd (*reading*)   Follow this line ... (*He follows a line, moving slowly.*) You are now pissing on your foot.

Eric   Rearrange this well-known phrase. Shit Mrs Thatcher is a ...

Ralph   I've got it! Mrs Shit is a Thatcher.

Judd   Don't be stupid. It's . . . Shit Thatcher, Mrs is a . . .

Les   Here's one: save water, piss on a friend.

They start to look at one another's genitals.

Eric (*to* **Ralph**)   What the hell is that?

Ralph   It's mine.

Eric   Jesus Christ!

Judd   What's up?

Eric   Look at that.

Judd   Bloody hell.

Ralph   What's the matter with you lot?

Eric (*to* **Les**)   Hey, seen this?

Les   What?

Eric   Look at that I've never seen one so big.

Les   Bleeding hell.

Ralph   Haven't you seen one before?

Eric   It's like a baby's arm with an orange in its fist.

Ralph   Let's have a look at yours then?

Eric   Gerraway you pervert.

Judd   It's not natural.

Les   It's an offensive weapon is that, he could mug somebody with it.

Ralph   Oh yeah?

Les   Come on let's get back on the dance floor.

They all zip up their trousers. **Ralph** *has buttons.*

Eric   Do you fancy a bit of a laugh?

All   Yeah . . . (*Laughter.*)

Music: Carmina Burana. *Suddenly they are bouncers once more.*

Les   Are we going inside or what?

Ralph   Eager tonight Les?

Les   I want to watch the skirt. I wanna see all them buttocks, shit I wanna talk to 'em.

Ralph   You want to talk to some buttocks?

Judd   He'll talk to anything.

Les   Just what do you say to women in here? How do you chat 'em up?

Ralph   You just start talking to them, an opening gambit.

Les   Like what?

Judd   Shut up and get your tits out?

Les   Subtle.

Ralph   Something like that.

Les   Mind you this is better than over-25s night.

Ralph   The floorboards creak and out come the creeps.

Les   Dripping in wall-to-wall cellulite.

Judd   Eric's favourite.

Ralph   Over-25s night?

Les   Grab-a-granny night.

Judd   He's looking for a woman aren't you Eric?

Eric   Shut up you.

Judd   Can't keep one when he's got one, doesn't know how to treat them. I think I saw your ex-wife down here on Tuesday, Eric.

Ralph Leave it Judd.

Judd And she wasn't alone.

Eric Shuddup.

Judd With a couple of young blokes I think.

Les Judd leave it.

Eric I'll have you.

Judd Oh yeah?

Ralph Leave it.

Judd No.

Eric I will have you Judd.

Judd I don't think so.

Eric I will.

Judd Come on then.

Eric Don't set me off.

Judd Come on.

Eric Don't Judd. Just don't.

Silence.

All Lucky Eric's second speech.

Eric On Tuesdays it's over-25s night. Mutton-dressed-as-lamb night, mutton-dressed-as-anything night. Sad night. And you can see the baggage they're bringing, husband dead, wife left him, divorced, run off, left him for the milkman. Or the businessman with a night to kill and a face full of lager. Skin bursting at the seams with alcohol, desperate for an illicit fling before returning to the wife to speak of a dull night in Wakefield, nothing to do, 'Yes dear, went to bed at half ten.' And the fire doors tell their secret stories.

Used prophylactics, tons of them, a mountain of
condoms and pitta bread behind the disco. Durex lay
like dead Smurfs, a symbol of a battle won, a conquest
taken, another victory against a hairdresser from
Garforth. And the pissed-up pale-faced lager-lousy lager
louts strut their funky stuff, attempting to pick up
something twice their age, for fun? For a laugh? And
the skeletons of their pasts float away, drunk on a
mixture of sweat and Southern Comfort. And she's
there, the wife is there, the ex-wife is there. In the
hunt, on the dance floor, moving awkwardly amongst
the anarchy they call dancing. And the pissed-up pale
face chats to her, touches her. I wish they'd start it
with me, I wish they'd start something with me. I wish
one of those skinny balmy bastards would just start it
with me. Just start it with me. Just let them start it
with me . . .

Eric *is near to breakdown. The other bouncers watch him with
some glee. Music plays. Slowly* **Judd**, **Les** *and* **Ralph** *exit.
The spotlight fades on* **Eric***.*

Act Two

Ralph, **Judd** *and* **Les** *enter and form a line, centre stage.*
Lucky Eric *joins the line, inspecting the audience.*

Judd (*to audience*) What are you laughing at?

Eric Do you think they're ready for it?

Les No. But they're gonna get it.

Loud disco music plays. **Ralph** *becomes the DJ once again.*
The others become the lads, by now fairly drunk, attempting to
dance while the DJ speaks.

Ralph Yeah! Wow! Things are really happening
down here tonight. Have some fun, yeah have some
fun. Tell you what girls . . . tell you what we'll do . . .
the first girl who brings me a matching pair of bra and
knickers, yes a pair of knickers and a bra, there'll be a
bottle of Asti Spumante and a fortnight's free entry, get
it, entry, to Mr Cinders. So come on girls, get them
off and bring them up to me, marvellous Michael Dee,
the DJ with the big B . . . (*Back outside.*) I think that the
snot up my nose is frozen.

Eric Very interesting.

Ralph Aren't you cold?

Eric No, I've got blood in my veins, not water.

Judd All fat, that's why.

Eric Listen what's talking.

Judd That's muscle.

Eric That's shit.

Ralph That's enough.

Eric Roll on two o'clock.

Judd Have we got any films in?

Les   Yeah. A bluey, it'll make your nose run, it's that blue.

Judd   Where did you get it?

All   Video shop.

Scene changes to the video shop. **Eric** *and* **Ralph** *are looking for videos.* **Judd** *plays the shop assistant.*

Les   Have you got any of them video nasties?

Judd   No, no, no, no . . . YES.

Les   Oh . . . what have you got?

Judd   I've got *Rambo One, Rambo Two, Rambo Three* to thirty-seven, *Friday the Thirteenth, Friday the Fifteenth, Monday the Twenty-third, October the Ninth, My Mother's Birthday, Bank Holiday Sunday* and most of the religious holidays in 3-D.

Ralph   *Queen Kong,* the story of a sixty-four-foot gay gorilla.

Les   Yes that's it, something a bit blue.

Judd   I've got light blue, dark blue, sky blue, and navy blue.

Les   Navy blue?

Judd   Or something with animals . . .

They all grunt and gurgle like animals.

Les   I'll take the one with animals. The boys should enjoy this.

Back outside the club.

Eric   Perverts . . .

Judd   At two o'clock the disco shuts . . . free drinks all round.

Les   At least we've got a video now.

Ralph   Yeah, you can say that again.

Les   At least we've got a video now.

Judd   Which beats the old projector we used to have, three-quarters of an hour fixing up the bloody projector. Then with sweaty hand in tight polyester, we'd watch the twitchin' and the screamin'. Like fish in a barrel, we'd fidget and jump watching plot and orifice explored.

All the bouncers have a drink. They then mime setting up the projector, ready to watch the blue movie. **Ralph** *and* **Eric** *act out the film.* **Eric** *plays a buxom Swede taking her clothes off, about to have a shower.* **Ralph** *plays the postman. Sleazy background music and strobe lights should give the scene a cinematic feel. The other bouncers provide a commentary.*

Ralph (*as though the doorbell*)   Bing bong . . .

Eric   Whom de iz eet?

Ralph   It ist me. Nobby, ze Swedish postman . . .

Les   Hey up. It's Nobby, Swedish postman.

Eric   Come on ze in, Nobby. I'm unt der shopwer, unt . . .

Les (*excitedly*)   Go on, Nobby lad . . .

Ralph   Ver ist der usband?

Eric   Engagedist unt ont dert buziness . . .

Les   Husband away on business . . .

Judd   Go on, Nob!

Eric   I am zo lonely wit my usband in Oslo . . .

Les   Aye, aye . . . she's lonely with her husband away on business in Oslo. I can understand that. Can you Judd? A woman alone and all that.

Judd   Gerron with the film.

Eric Oh. I've dropped the soapen on the flooren.

Ralph She's dropped the soapen on the flooren.

Les She's dropped the soap.

Judd Go on . . . Nobby, my son . . .

*As Nobby (**Eric**) is about to move the action freezes as if the film has jammed. Strobe stops.*

Judd Give that projector a boot.

All Boot!

Strobe re-starts. The action is now played in reverse, as though the film is being rewound, up to the doorbell ringing at the start. We snap out of this scene and the actors are all bouncers again.

Judd It's not fair.

Eric Porno films . . . a waste of time.

Judd It pays your wages.

Les There's something wrong with a bloke who doesn't enjoy a good bluey, that's what I say.

Ralph I think that's a fair comment, Les.

Judd Eric doesn't like them. He thinks it's degrading.

Les What's degrading about it – they get paid for it. I mean it's not exactly as if they're doing it for peanuts.

Judd I'd do it for peanuts. I'd do it for one peanut . . . Eh? What a job? It's not exactly a matter of being a good actor is it? Just get in there, get stripped off, get stuck in . . . Not a bad job Eric, eh? Beats this shit.

Eric You're an animal, Judd.

Judd Keep talking . . .

Eric An animal . . .

Judd How's that?

Eric Don't you know?

All (*very softly*) Lucky Eric's third speech.

As **Eric** *speaks, the others can act out the scene. Background music should play.*

Eric I'm sat in this pub, just an ordinary pub, and it's Christmas. Everybody's had one over the eight. And there's a group of lads, football supporters, that type, eleven stone, walking about like they think they're Frank Bruno. And there's this girl nineteen, twenty, and she's drunk, and she's got it all there, the figure, the looks. The lads are laughing, joking with her. 'Give us a kiss eh?' And she does. Well, it's Christmas, I think, well, it is Christmas. I sat watching for an hour. She was well pissed; they all had a go, kissing her, feeling her, lifting her skirt up. Nobody noticed, pub was packed. Merry Christmas they'd say, and line up for another kiss and a feel, each one going further than the other, until I could see the tops of her thighs bare. And in that pub, she had them all, or they had her, six of 'em, in a pub. Nobody noticed, nobody noticed but me. It was a strange feeling, a weird feeling, I remember walking over to where they were. I was aroused more than ever before in my life. I'm so powerful, so powerful. I stood in front of them, looking at them. The first head was quite hard, but the others were soft, like eggs; they hit the wall and smashed. The girl stood up. 'Give us a kiss,' she said, 'give us a kiss.' 'Go home,' I said, 'please go home . . .'

Lights come up.

Les So what's the plan then?

Judd Inside?

Les Yeah.

Ralph The usual.

Les What if there's a big fight, rush in, eh? Get

some kicks in.

Eric   Don't be a twat all your life, Les. Have a night off.

Les   A few kicks never hurt anybody.

Judd   Look at all those lights . . . them lights are like people . . . they are like people's lights . . .

Eric   Anybody could do this job.

Les   Bollocks!

Eric   No they could, it's a matter of ego.

Les   Isn't that Frankenstein's mate?

Ralph   That's Igor.

Les   Same innit?

Eric   His brain's painted on.

Les   But he's handy though, Eric.

Eric   I'm telling you. It's all image.

Ralph   Eric's got a point. I once heard some talk of a nightclub in Manchester that employed a woman.

Judd   Bollocks . . .

Les   Pull the other one . . .

Ralph   Straight up is this; she was a big fat woman.

Judd   I know her.

Ralph   Whenever somebody was making an arsehole of themselves, she'd go over and tell 'em not to be so stupid, tell them to pull themselves together. She never had any trouble either.

Judd   Can't see that happening down here; she'll probably get glassed.

Les   Or picked up.

All   HA HA HA.

Inside the disco. **Ralph** *becomes Suzy,* **Eric** *becomes Baz,* **Les** *becomes Kev and* **Judd** *becomes Elaine.*

Eric   It's ten past one. Baz is well gone.

Les   Kev is ready to try it on, with anyone with two legs and two tits. Two teeth, anything.

Judd   Plain Elaine has got a pain in her head, she's ready for bed.

Ralph   Suzy is sexy, she's been flirting about.

Eric   What about those two? Come on let's get in, have a bash.

Les   Just give a sec. I'm dying for a slash.

Les *moves off.* **Eric** *(Baz) now walks up to the girls.*

Eric   Now then girls, alright are we?

Judd   Piss off fatty.

Eric   You can't get around me that easy.

Judd   You're ugly.

Eric   That's nice. What's your name?

Ralph   Suzy. I'm drunk you know?

Eric   Wanna have a dance?

Ralph   What about my friend?

Eric   I've got a mate, he's just gone for a slash, he'll be back in a dash. Come on shall we go . . .

Judd   Hey, I hope I'm not gonna be left here?

Ralph   I'm only going for a dance, Elaine, that's all.

Eric *and* **Ralph** *move upstage as if to the dance floor and freeze.* **Les** *comes back from the toilet, and is faced with* **Judd** *(Elaine).*

Les   Where's Baz?

Judd   Is he fat?

Les   A bit.

Judd   He's just got off with my friend.

Les   The lucky gett! Go on, pole it. He always gets the pretty ones.

Judd   D'you wanna dance?

Les   Who me?

Judd   Come on, I like you.

Les   Gerroff me.

Both couples now take up a smooching position. They begin to think aloud.

Eric   God! She smells great, her chest's really warm. I can just about feel her arse. I think she's drunk. Oh no, I'm gerrin' a hard-on. She's rubbin' herself against me.

Eric *moves his body in order to dance away from* **Ralph** *(Suzy).*

Ralph   I don't know where I am, I'm sinking and spinning, round and round, round and round . . .

Judd   So am I.

Les   This is bad news, I hope nobody sees me. I think Terry's drunk anyway. She's strong is this one. She's breaking my bleeding back. I just hope that she doesn't fall over. I can feel her fat.

Judd   If he makes a move or tries anything with me I'll break his arms. He's nice and cute though, I'll say that much. I think he likes me . . .

Les   She is the ugliest girl I've ever met . . .

Eric   I think I've pulled a cracker this time . . .

Ralph I'll let him take me home but I'm not having sex.

Eric I bet she goes like a rabbit.

Ralph I do.

Les I hope she doesn't try and kiss me. I'll spew.

Eric Wait while I tell all the lads.

Ralph His breath smells awful, I think he must smoke.

Eric Yes, I'm in here, no trouble.

Ralph He's really too big, a bit of a joke. He's not what I'm after, not handsome and slim. I'll tell him I'm going to the loo, that should lose him . . . I'll have to nip to the toilet.

Eric You what?

Ralph I've got to go to the toilet.

Eric What for?

Ralph Don't be nosey.

Eric Don't be long, will yer?

Ralph You wait here, don't move. I'll be back in a tick.

Eric Right.

Ralph *walks away from* **Eric**. **Eric** *freezes as he looks at his watch.*

Les Listen.

Judd What?

Les I'll have to go now.

Judd Why?

Les I should have turned into a pumpkin ten

minutes ago.

Judd Oh yeah.

Les Look can you let me go please . . .

Judd Give me a kiss first . . .

Les I can't.

Judd Why?

Les I've got something that I don't want you to catch.

Judd What's that?

Les Me. I've got a terminal disease.

Judd You haven't. You're only saying that.

Les Like fuck I am.

Judd You're stopping here with me, or I'll chop your face off.

Les Look get off me you fat overweight disgusting horrible smelly fat slag.

Music plays. 'Feed The World'. Slowly **Judd** *exits. As he does* **Ralph***, furious, comes to* **Les**.

Ralph Hey shit-breath, what have you been saying about our lass?

Les I haven't been saying anything.

Ralph You have . . . I heard you at the bar.

Les Look twat, don't start. There's three of us.

Ralph Don't start with me twat, there's three of us.

Ralph *kicks* **Les** *in the bollocks. He falls.* **Judd** *and* **Eric** *enter. They stop the fight.*

All (*shout*) FIGHT!

They all now dash to the centre of the stage, as bouncers and

*lads, grab each other and generally give the impression that there
is a fight going on.*

Eric Come on you two. Leave it out. Get them out,
Judd. Fire exit.

Judd Let's do the bastards.

Eric Let's just get them out.

Judd I'm going to do mine.

Eric Don't.

Judd Who are you talking to Eric?

Eric You, you daft bastard.

Judd Oh yeah.

Ralph Hey no need to fight over us lads.

Eric Piss off . . . There's no need to do them over,
just leave them. They're pissed up anyway.

Judd Who do you think you are, Eric?

Eric Nobody.

Judd You get up my back.

Eric Look, Judd, don't set me off.

Judd You weird bastard!

Eric I said, don't set me off.

Judd You shouldn't be doing this job. You should be
bouncing at Mothercare. You're soft.

Eric Don't set me off.

Judd Soft inside.

Eric Don't set me . . .

Judd Soft bastard.

Eric *turns on* **Judd**, *forces him to the ground and almost* *breaks his arm.* **Judd** *lies protrate,* **Les** *and* **Ralph** *run to the scene,* **Eric** *makes a threat against the two of them.*

Eric Come on, come on, I'll have you and all.

Ralph Eric, it's me, it's Ralph, it's me.

Eric Sorry, Judd, sorry.

Judd *slowly gets to his feet and walks upstage with* **Les**. *Both of them speak together.*

Judd/Les Lucky Eric's fourth and final speech.

Spotlight on **Eric**.

Eric We have these Miss Wet T-shirt and Miss Instring evenings. Eighteen-year-old beauties displaying their orbs through string vests or firm outlines on wet cotton, naked some of them, save their skimpy knickers. All of them somebody's daughters, mothers some of them, my wife, one of them. And the glossy polaroids on the doors outside show more hideous topless antics. Breasts in beer glasses, breasts smeared in shaving foam, breasts oiled and on show. And Michael Dee the DJ kisses and sucks as if they were his own, slimy bastard. I see the girls selling themselves for five minutes' fame. I can see the staid state of exploitation, I can even smell the peaches of their underarm roll-on. The working class with no options left, exposing its weakness. I feel very sad. I feel very protective, I might pack it all in. I might pack it all in, fuck off, go home and listen to Elvis Presley.

Music plays. A spotlight picks out **Ralph** *as Michael Dee.*

Ralph Someone has just handed me a piece of paper from the dance floor and on it it asks me to dedicate this next record to Sharon and Darren who are out there getting it together. So tell him you love him Shaz, and tell her you love her, Davs. After all a little white lie never really hurt anyone did it . . . but let's be serious for a moment shall we. All of you girls out there tonight at Mr Cinders, later on when you're really getting it together spare a thought for me, and for our doormen, who couldn't even pull a muscle. And I know one of them who will certainly be going home, lonesome tonight.

Eric   You're dead pal.

Ralph   Just a joke Eric, so remember me, Marvellous Michael Dee, your love doctor.

Judd   Witch doctor.

Elvis plays: 'Are You Lonesome Tonight'. **Eric**, **Judd**, **Les** *sway.* **Ralph** *exits and enters upstage. The feel of a dream is conveyed.*

Les   How's the wife Eric?

Eric   Left me.

Judd   How are the kids Eric?

Eric   She took them with her.

Les   I hear she's seeing another bloke.

Eric   He's in the Merchant Navy.

Les   Bit of a fat bastard.

Judd   Yeah I know him.

Ralph   It's ten to two. Let's get back on the door.

Les   Yeah. Nothing left now, only the dogs.

Ralph   Coyote women.

Les   What?

Ralph   Coyote women. A woman you take to bed tonight and love, but in the morning you see she's so ugly, and she's laid on your arm, that rather than wake her up you bite your own arm off. Coyote women.

Les There's a lot of ugly men as well Ralph.

Ralph Don't look at me when you say that.

Judd My arm hurts, I think he's broke my arm.

Eric I just sit in the flat waiting for the night time, waiting for the night to come around. Waiting for something to happen.

Ralph Wanderlust.

Les What is?

Ralph That's why we're all here. Maybe tonight. Maybe this time we'll meet Sister Right. Maybe this time she'll be a nice girl. And it goes on and on. Wanderlust.

Judd My other arm's alright though.

Eric I'm just sat all day, in the dark, in the flat, in the cold, waiting, waiting for her, waiting for the kids, waiting for something to tell me I'm alive.

Ralph Wanderlust.

Judd Let's go outside and nut some bastard.

The bouncers howl like werewolves. 'Three Times A Lady' can be heard. Suddenly we are in the disco with the lads.

Ralph I was right you know?

Eric What d'you mean?

Ralph There are only ugly 'uns left at two o'clock.

Eric I had one, but she walked off.

Les Was she drunk?

Judd Must have been.

Eric Thanks.

Les What about them four, over there?

Ralph You what? She must weigh about seventeen stones.

Eric Better than nothing.

Les She'd eat me.

Judd She'd eat us all.

Eric What do you say to someone that big?

Les Sod off. You're big.

Judd Sod off, ya pig.

Others No no no. He said big . . .

Judd Sod off ya big pig . . . it wasn't me that said that, it was me brother . . . and I haven't even got a brother . . .

Les You have, he's in *Star Trek* . . . You're right you know, there are only scrag-ends left at two o'clock.

Judd Sod you lot, I'm game.

Les *puts a paper bag on his head.*

All And me.

The lads begin to dance with imaginary women.

Ralph Hey you don't sweat much for a big girl do you?

Eric Can I borrow your face? I'm going ratting tomorrow.

Les Do you want a drink? The bar's over there.

Judd Give us a kiss, come on . . .

Ralph Didn't I used to go to school with you?

Les Does your Dad race pigeons . . . ?

Eric Does your shit stink?

All Oooooooohhhh.

Slowly the lads change back to the bouncers. It is closing time and the bouncers encourage people to leave, see them off, etc.

Eric   Goodnight.

Les   'Night love, take care.

Judd   Goodnight.

Ralph   'Night . . .

Eric   Take it nice and steady.

Les (*looking at an imaginary woman*)   Look at the arsehole on that.

Ralph   She's had a skinful . . .

Judd   She's got handles on her hips.

Les *becomes a punter, leaving the disco.*

Les   I've had a great night, fellas . . . I've had a wonderful evening.

Eric   Come away from him, mate.

Les   Does anyone know where I can get another bottle of champagne?

Eric   You've had enough.

Les   Just one more bottle of champers, and everything will be tickety-tickety-boo.

Judd   Tickety-tickety-fucking-boo. Watch this, I'll nut him.

Eric   Leave him.

Les   Goodnight.

Les (*as a bouncer*)   Yeah goodnight, sir.

Judd   Watch this, I'll nut him.

Eric   Goodnight.

Ralph   Have a safe journey home.

Les *becomes a bouncer once more.*

Les   Goodnight. She's down here every night is that one.

Judd   I thought I'd seen her before.

Les   She's been hanging around me like flies around shit.

Eric   You said that Les, not us.

Les   I think she's after something.

Ralph   Eat shit, five million flies can't be wrong.

Les   What?

Eric   Nice to hear that old one again. Goodnight, love.

All   Goodnight, goodnight, goodnight.

Eric   And at two thirty around the back of the disco.

Les   You can hear the heavy breathing ...

Ralph   The gasping and the sighing ...

Judd   The unzipping and the fumbling ...

Eric   And there she is, Sexy Suzy, having drunk a bathful of Bacardi, being felt and groped by a foul-mouthed tattooed coil of muscle from Leeds.

Les   And he tugs and fumbles and feels and fingers and pokes ...

Ralph   And soaks her with sloppy kisses, the neck, the ears, the cleavage.

Judd   And the elastic of her knickers snaps in the night, and he's inside her. Pumping.

Les   Groaning ... Hard.

Ralph   Pushing, hard.

Judd   Grabbing her hard.

Les   Losing his footing on the asphalt.

Eric   And Sexy Suzy, spins, and feels nothing, he pushes hard, gasping, scratching, sweating, and in her nothingness she eats a cold pizza. Delicately like a lady at a summer ball she picks at this pizza pepperoni.

Ralph   And he still pumps.

Eric   And she still eats.

Les   And he still pumps and grasps, and slops kisses on her neck.

Judd   And she still eats the pizza.

Les   And when he finally arrives, with a gasp of bad ale-smelling breath, a burp of an orgasm, he stands, legs shaking like a shitting dog, and he says . . .

Judd   . . . that was fucking brilliant.

Eric   And she finishes her feast, and discards the pizza box amongst the piles of condoms and pitta bread. And don't tell us that it's not true, 'cos we've seen it, don't tell us that it's disgusting because we've smelt the awful stench. Don't tell us that it's all that they deserve, just tell us why . . . Tell us why?

Suddenly **Eric**, **Judd** *and* **Ralph** *become the lads singing.*

All   Here we go, here we go, here we go, here we go . . .

Scene change to the lads now waiting for a taxi.

Eric   Baz –

Judd   Terry –

Ralph   Jerry –

Les   Kev

All   Waaaaaaaaaaaaay!

Judd Have you seen the length of this taxi queue? I'm friggin' freezin'.

Les I wish I'd've put a big coat on.

Ralph Oh no, look at that . . . I've got spew all over me shoe.

Les I have.

Judd I have.

Eric I've got shit on mine.

All Waaaaayyyy!

Judd Innit dark?

Les Well it is half-past three.

Judd Half-past bloody three and we're stood out in the cold freezin' to bloody death.

Eric Just think, if I'd've got off with that Suzy I'd be in bed now snuggling up to her brown, tanned, sunburnt soft body.

All Whaaaaaaaaaaaaaaay!

Les Innit quiet? All asleep, and tucked away in their little boxes. Innit quiet? Listen, listen to the city. Quiet, innit? All those people asleep. It's like being in a painting.

Judd Is it bollocks.

Eric I'm dying for a slash.

Ralph Do you feel pissed up?

Judd Who?

Ralph You?

Judd (*considering the possibility*) No. Not now.

Ralph No, I don't.

Judd I did about an hour ago. I've sobered up I think.

Les It's the cold.

Eric I'm having a slash. (*He begins to urinate.*)

Les (*pretending a taxi approaches*) TAXI!

Eric Oh shit! (*He attempts to do up his flies.*)

Les Only a joke.

Judd I've spent thirty-five quid.

Ralph Yeah?

Judd Jesus Christ, I've spent thirty-five bleeding quid.

Ralph I have.

Judd That had to last me till Wednesday.

Eric Feel better after that slash.

Judd Thirty-five quid! I didn't even get a kiss or a feel of tit. Pissing hell, I'm depressed.

Ralph We all are.

All Social comment?

Les Alright, it's up to you ... I've spent forty quid, next week's board money. My mam'll have a fit.

Eric I've spent ... er ... I've forgot what I came out with. I've only got thirty-seven pence left.

Judd Yeah, but thirty-five quid.

Ralph (*hails a taxi*) Taxi! St John's Flats ... waaaaaaay!

Les Hey look, it's them four birds!

Whoops of delight as the taxi arrives. They mime getting into the taxi and it screeches off. They sit moving as though in a car. One of the lads lights a cigarette and begins to smoke. One of the others begins to feel sick.

Ralph   I feel sick.

The actors convey the sensation that the car is speeding away and taking corners at fast speed. **Ralph** *begins to retch.*

Ralph   Tell him to stop.

Eric   I want another slash.

Ralph   Tell him to stop or I'm gonna be sick.

Judd (*as though speaking to the driver*)   Will you stop? He says he's not stopping 'cos it might be a trick.

Eric   A trick? What's he want me to do? Rupture my bladder?

Les   I feel a bit spewy. Tell him to slow down.

Ralph   Tell him to stop.

Judd   I've told him.

Les   Let some air in here. It's like a wrestler's jock-strap.

Eric *urinates out of the window. It all blows back into the others' faces.*

Eric   I'm doing it out of the window.

Les   Don't be so bloody stupid.

Eric   Hey lads, I'm slashing out of the window...

Ralph   Errm... I've been sick down his back.

Judd   Window... dick... SHUT! (*He shuts the window.*)

Eric   Aaaaaargh!

The car suddenly screeches to a halt. Scene switches back to the bouncers at the club.

Ralph   Look at the bleeding mess.

Eric Animals.

Judd *sings nonsense into the microphone.*

Les Look at the amount of beer that's been left. A waste is that, waste.

They stand around contemplating the mess.

Judd Shall we get packed away and get the video on?

Eric Eager tonight Judd, aren't you?

Judd I wanna see the filth.

Eric You are too sensitive Judd, that's your problem.

Ralph Look at the mess. Hey there's a pair of knickers over here.

Les Keep 'em, they might fit you.

Judd I'll give you one pound twelve for 'em.

Eric Have you seen the bogs?

Les What's wrong with them?

Eric Two urinals cracked, it's all over the floor.

Judd What is?

Ralph *(still rummaging around)* Anybody want a basket meal? One here, still warm.

Eric Ah ah . . . look at this.

Les What?

Eric Another fiver.

Judd Jammy bastard.

Eric That's four nights on the trot.

Ralph That's why they call him 'Lucky' Eric.

Judd Are we gerrin' this video on or what?

Eric   He is a pervert.

Ralph   Well I don't know about you lads, but I'm shagged.

Les   And me.

Judd   I wish I was.

Eric   I wish you was and all Judd.

Ralph   I'll tell you this much Eric, I don't think I can stand much more of this. It's getting to me. It's all bloody getting to me.

Eric (*challenges strongly*)   That's because you're soft . . .

Silence.

Ralph (*doesn't respond*)   Innit peaceful. Listen how quiet it is.

Judd   My ears are still buzzing.

Eric   My brain's buzzing. I think I'm going deaf.

Les   You what?

Eric   I said I think I'm . . . oh very funny lads. You lads are definitely on the ball at this late hour.

Judd   Are we gerrin' this video on or what?

Les   Yeah Ralph get some cans, we'll have a couple of hours. Are you stopping Eric?

Eric   No I'm not a pervert.

Judd   Ha ha. Look at that. Twenty pence. And it's mine. Look he's dying to stop.

Eric   I wanna get off home.

Judd   Just watch the first bit.

Eric   No I . . .

Les   Come on . . .

Eric No, I'm not stopping.

Judd Come on Eric, spoil yourself.

Les Yeah, come on.

Eric No, I . . .

Judd Come on, man . . .

Eric Well, OK. I'll stop for the first three hours.

Judd Right. Where's that video with animals in it?

Les Right. Let's get it on.

They put on the imaginary video. It is Michael Jackson's Thriller. *Music comes up and the lights fade to green, as the bouncers all don monster's teeth. They proceed to do a complicated rip-off of the* Thriller *video, moving forwards and backwards, grotesquely slouching their shoulders, clapping their hands, etc. (NB: The* Thriller *video should be carefully studied in order to achieve just the right elements of parody.) Eventually the lights come up and the music stops.*

Judd Who brought that fucking video?

Les I did.

Judd I thought you said it had animals in it.

Les It did have animals in it.

Judd I thought it was shit.

Ralph Thanks Barry Norman.

The music from the start of the play comes up again.

Eric
  Down at the disco was the place to be
  The lights were so bright
  Like a colour TV
  The music was loud
  And the beer flowed free
  It was a disco place for you and me

On the door you paid your money
The place was packed
The place was funny
You saw the girls
Mmmmmmmm . . . smelled their honey

The heads were hazy
The limbs were lazy
And all the young girls
Dance like crazy
Come on

But now it's over you gotta go home
There is nowhere else to roam
Be careful how you walk the streets
They're the meanest streets
In the whole damn place
It's a real mean street
For the human race.

And through the blood
And snot and sex
Maybe lovers meet
And are married next
Two spirits moved
To hold and cling
And the children of England
They still sing

All

Here we go, here we go, here we go
Here we go, here we go, here we go
Here we go, here we go, here we go

Well Friday nights and Saturdays too
We'll be down here, yes with you and you
And the whole damn crew
Is there anything else to do

I said a hip hop
A hippy a hippy

A hip hip hop
And don't you stop!

Blackout.

Happy Families

Happy Families was commissioned by British Telecom for the Little Theatre Guild of Great Britain and received 49 simultaneous premières by members of the Guild in October 1991. The play was subsequently rewritten and performed professionally at the West Yorkshire Playhouse in February 1992, with the following cast:

John	Nick Lane
Dot	Judith Barker
Vic	Andrew Livingstone
Liz	Marcia Warren
Jack	Wilfred Grove
Aunty Doris	Jane Clifford
Aunty Edna	Maggie Lane
Rebecca	Henrietta Voigts
Lyn Sutton	Henrietta Voigts

Directed by John Godber
Designed by Rob Jones

Act One

A living-room. The room is carpeted and painted cream, its features blurred slightly, as if seen in memory; it is not realistic, but quite definitely a theatrical set. There is an exit upstage left. Centre is a sofa; other furniture is set out in appropriate positions.

As the play begins, music from the late nineteen sixties is playing. The cast enter and take up positions around the stage. **John** *sits on the sofa; he is wearing a suit for his university graduation.* **Dot** *begins to clean the floor with a vacuum cleaner (which has no lead); she is dressed in clothes from the nineteen sixties.*

The music fades. **Vic** *enters.*

Vic She's at it again.

Dot What?

Vic Look at you.

Dot I want it to be nice for your Edna coming. (*She stops cleaning the floor and begins to polish the furniture.*)

John (*to the audience*) My mother was cleaning, as usual, and my dad stood watching her in disbelief. She'd already hoovered that part of the carpet a hundred times.

Vic Do you have to go crackers every day?

John (*to the audience*) She did, it was a disease.

Vic I mean you're nearly through to the floorboards.

John (*to the audience*) But my dad had learnt to live with her; my mother would always tell him:

Dot You can't plan housework. A house has a life of its own. I don't work shifts, Vic, I'm on call all the time. Now go and put the kettle on . . .

Vic   It won't fit me.

John (*to the audience*)   My dad's jokes were only funny once, but he told them a thousand times.

Vic   Dot, this Indian right, walks into a trading post, 'Oh, my head.' Trading post, wood, get it, a wooden post?

Jack *enters slowly, carrying a pair of garden clippers. He is a strong, dour character.*

Jack   These garden clippers need sharpening, Vic.

Vic   Right-oh, Pa.

Vic *exits with clippers.*

John (*to the audience*)   And then there was my grandad, who was a real myth. He was a maniac and would fight any man, anywhere.

Liz *enters the scene. She has a duster in her hand.*

Liz   Have you finished them hedges?

Jack   Ar.

Liz   Have you made a good job?

Jack   Ar.

Liz   Go and cut the lawns.

Jack   Ar.

Jack *silently exits.* **Liz** *is left, flicking her duster.*

John (*to the audience*)   My grandmother was a bundle of love and affection. She had bone cancer in later life but she never told anyone.

Liz   I think I'll have a cuppa tea, Doris.

Liz *exits.* **Doris** *enters, knitting.*

Doris   It's brewing, Mam, I'm just seeing to it.

John (*to the audience*)   This is my Aunty Doris, she's my mucky aunty.

Doris   I'm knitting our John another tank top, nip.

Dot (*off*)   Lovely.

Doris *exits.* **Edna** *enters, sipping her tea.*

John (*to the audience*)   My Aunty Doris knitted constantly, but she had a problem with sizes.

Edna   This is lovely. It really is lovely tea, Dorothy. Is it Rington's?

John (*to the audience*)   My posh Aunty Edna lived in Gloucester. She'd left Yorkshire and married a man from Cambridge. She worked with cancer patients all her life and was a cut above the rest.

Edna   It's a long drive but we like to make the effort to come 'home'.

Rebecca, *aged eleven, enters. She carries a clarinet.*

Rebecca   I like going to see Aunty Dot and Uncle Vic, they're so sweet.

Edna   Go on, Rebecca, play something.

John (*to the audience*)   Rebecca was my cousin. She was supposed to be a child genius.

Edna *and* **Rebecca** *exit,* **Rebecca** *playing 'You Make Me Feel So Young' appallingly as she goes.* **Dot** *begins to hum the tune.*

John (*to the audience*)   It was nineteen sixty-seven. And in nineteen sixty-seven I was waiting for a letter that would shape my life for ever.

John *exits.* **Dot** *sings a verse of 'You Make Me Feel So Young'.* **Vic** *enters. He is carrying a letter and is very excited.*

Vic   It's here. It's here.

Dot   Settle down, you'll have a bloody stroke. (*She stops cleaning.*)

Vic   It's here, it's come. I've just seen t' postwoman.

Dot   Well, open it.

Vic   I'm shaking.

Dot   Give it to me.

Vic   No, I want to read it. I've been waiting for this to come. Where is he? Is he in t' garden?

Dot   He's kicking that ball about.

Vic   Shout him in.

Dot   Look at you, you're like a big kid, now stop getting over-excited. (*She shouts.*) John? John, what are you doing, where are you?

John, *dressed in shorts and a very large tank top, enters.*

Vic   Your letter's come, kid. Results from school.

Dot   Well, open it, we haven't got all day.

John (*to the audience*)   I'm eleven and I'm bloody nervous.

Vic (*opening the letter*)   Here we are ... (*He reads.*) 'Dear Mr and ...' Yeah, blah blah. Here we are ... 'to inform you that John has been successful in achieving a place at ...' (*His voice changes; he sounds desperately disappointed.*) '*Clifton Secondary Modern School.* Term commences September the thirteenth, nineteen sixty-seven.'

There is a silence.

Dot   Right.

Vic   Oh, well ...

Another silence.

Dot (*with a massive sigh*)   Oh, dear . . .

Another silence.

Vic   Shall we get cleaned up?

Dot   We'd better. Oh, John.

John (*to* **Dot**)   What does it mean, Mam?

Dot   It means you're not going to grammar school. Come here, what are we going to make of you, eh?

Vic   It means you've failed, kid. Failed your eleven-plus.

John   I can't even remember taking it.

Vic   Typical of our John, he can't even remember taking it, he probably didn't take it. I bet he was playing bloody football that day.

Dot (*slowly*)   I could belt him.

Vic   Don't start it . . .

Dot   I could . . .

Vic   Leave him alone.

Dot   I could belt you, I could, Vic, he's got me all on edge.

Vic   Do you think I couldn't?

Dot   Well, belt him then.

Vic   You belt him.

Dot   You, my lad, you, you . . .

John   What?

Dot   You little thing . . .

Vic   Leave him.

Dot   A failure.

Vic   I said leave him.

Dot   Failed his eleven-plus, I just can't believe it.

Vic   I knew.

Dot   A failure.

Vic   He's not a failure.

Dot   Well, what is he then?

Vic   He's my lad.

Dot   He's my lad too.

Vic   I thought you were supposed to love him?

Dot   I do.

Vic   Well, shut up then.

John (*to the audience*)   They were right and I knew it. I was a failure. Thrown out at eleven. I think it made it worse when my family found out how many had passed.

Vic (*loudly*)   Two.

Dot   Don't go on.

Vic   Two.

Dot   If you say two again I'll scream.

Vic   Two. Two kids fail in a class of thirty-two and our John is one of them?

John (*to the audience*)   It was a good year.

Vic   And he's supposed to be intelligent. You said making him go to bed early would make him intelligent.

Dot   That's what my mother did with me.

Vic   And look at you.

Dot   I went to bed early every night.

Vic   So what?

Dot   Me and our Doris were always in bed by seven.

Vic   What's that got to do with the price of eggs?

Dot   And we got up early, not like you.

Vic   I get up before you.

Dot   Right, my lad, you will go to bed early for the rest of your life.

Vic   Too late now, isn't it?

Dot   He can go to bed early tonight, anyway.
There is a pause.

Vic   How come Denis Smeaton passed and he didn't, how come? His dad's a postman! How come Tony Baines passed? Lyn Sutton next door passed. Keith Eastmoor is going to be a dentist. Andrew West is going to be a vet. Mrs Thompson told me that her son is going to walk on the moon.

Dot   Don't be ridiculous.

Vic   How come they passed and he didn't?

Dot   He probably sat the wrong exam, knowing our John.

Vic *and* **Dot** *exit in silence.*

John *(to the audience)*   I knew I was a no-hoper. Two years earlier I'd been playing doctors and nurses next door with Lyn Sutton.

Lyn Sutton *enters. She is seven years old, a coy girl with a bow in her hair, short socks and a dress.*

Lyn   I've got a pain, Doctor.

John *(to the audience)*   I loved this game.

Lyn   I've got this pain. I've got an awful pain in my body.

John (*to* **Lyn**)   Where is it?

Lyn   On my body, Doctor.

John   Where, Nurse?

Lyn   Somewhere.

John   Is it here? (*He touches the top of her chest, very slowly and shyly.*)

Lyn   No.

John   Is it here? (*He moves his hand slowly down her chest.*)

Lyn   No, Doctor. It's not there. And it hurts me when I breathe.

John   Does it?

Lyn   Yes, it does.

John (*moving his hand to lightly touch her breast*)   Is it here?

Lyn   Yes. That's it, Doctor. That's much better.

John   Well, you had better take two tablets a day, Nurse, and if the pain comes back you had better come and see me again. Thank you. Next please.

Lyn   Now you.

John   What?

Lyn   Now you. Show me.

John   I haven't got any pains. Besides, I'm the doctor.

Lyn   Show me.

John   What?

Lyn   You know.

John   I don't.

Lyn   Your whatsit?

John   No.

Lyn   I've shown you mine.

John   Your what?

Lyn   Thing.

John   Oh yeah . . . urghhh.

Lyn   Come on . . . I'll be the doctor, and you come
and have to show me.

John   Oh, all right.

John *begins to take off his trousers, revealing British Home
Stores underwear. He prepares to show his manhood to* **Lyn** *but
. . .* **Dot** *enters, coming only a little way onstage.*

Dot   John! John!

John   (*grabbing at his trousers, panic-stricken*)   Oh no.

Dot   John, are you there? Tea's ready.

John   Yeah . . .

Dot   Your Aunty Edna's come to see us.

John   Oh crikey, oh no . . .

Dot *exits. The introduction to Alma Cogan's 'Hernando's
Hideaway' begins to play.* **John** *exits, attempting to put on his
trousers.* **Lyn** *exits in the opposite direction. The lights fade and
then come up on* **Edna**, **Dot**, **Vic** *and* **Doris** *having tea.*

Dot   Does anybody want any spring onion? Anybody?
Would you like some beetroot, Edna?

Edna   No thank you. I'm quite happy with this cup
of tea, Dorothy, thanks. Is it Rington's?

Dot   No, it's Typhoo. I got it from Denis Richards,
he's got a little shop on the corner. His mother's in a
wheelchair. They're really nice people. Wouldn't say

boo to a goose.

Edna Oh, I see.

Dot Would you like an Eccles cake?

Edna No thanks.

Dot They're nice.

Edna No, really.

Dot Are you sure?

Edna Positive. I've already had far too many.

Dot You've only had one.

Edna *does not answer, just sips her tea.*

Doris Does she want a tart? Give her a tart, our Dorothy, give her a tart. I've brought 'em; give her a tart. They're lovely.

John *enters, his trousers back-to-front. He stands looking shyly at his family.*

Edna No, honestly, I couldn't. Honestly.

Dot (*to* **John**) Say hello to your Aunty Edna, don't just stand there like a drip.

John (*whispering*) Hello.

Vic He's shy, Edna. Say hello proper.

John (*in the same voice*) Hello.

Edna Hello, John, nice to see you. How are you?

John *does not respond.*

Dot He's very shy.

Edna Are you. Are you shy?

John *nods.*

Doris He's lovely, aren't you? I could eat him. He's

a bit shy, Edna, but he'll grow out of it when he gets
a bit older. He's been playing next door, haven't you?
Been playing with the little girl next door. It's his
girlfriend, isn't it?

John No.

Doris He knows it is.

Edna Rebecca sends her apologies, John, she wanted
to come but her school have gone to Germany.
They've gone to Germany for ten days. I think they're
going to try and go ski-ing while they're out there.

Vic That sounds good, kid, eh?

Edna She's doing very well at the moment, Vic.

Vic Is she?

Edna She's doing *very well* at the moment.

Vic That's good to hear, isn't it, Dot?

Dot Doing well is she?

Edna She's doing very well. At the moment. We're
not quite sure how it's going to go, but fingers crossed.
This is really nice tea.

Dot It's Typhoo. It's not Kington's.

Edna *is transfixed by* **John** *having his trousers on back to
front.*

Edna John. I was just wondering if you knew that
you have your trousers on the wrong way around. Did
you know? They're on back to front? Did you know?

All the family have now become interested. **John** *fidgets and tries
to look innocent.*

John No.

Edna Well they are, unless they're rather special
trousers? Are they?

John   No.

Edna   Oh.

Doris   Oh, yeah they are ... It took me a minute to realise. He's probably made a mistake.

Vic   Did you know that, John?

John   Yeah. My gran bought them for me. They're new, they've got pockets in the back.

Dot   Turn around.

John   No.

Dot   Turn around.

John   Mam ... ?

Doris   Are they new? They're lovely, I think.

Dot   Turn around.

John *reluctantly turns round; we see that the fly and zip of his trousers are at the back.*

Doris   That's good, they've got a zip at the back. They're lovely.

Dot (*sinister*)   What have you been doing?

John   Eh.

Dot   Turn back around.

John *turns back to face his mother.*

Doris   I like the colour.

Dot   What have you been doing?

John   Nothing.

Dot   You have.

John   I haven't.

Dot   What have you been playing at in there?

John   Nothing.

Dot   Don't lie. If you lie I'll hit you. If you tell me the truth I'll let you off.

John   I haven't been doing nothing, Mam.

Vic (*whispering to* **Dot**)   Leave him. Do you want some more tea, Edna?

Edna   I'm fine.

Dot   What's been going on?

John (*steeling himself to tell the story; he acts it out rather badly*)   Well, it must have been a mistake, and when I pulled my trousers up, my body must have spun around and then it got stuck and I was facing the wrong way, and that must be what happened because my trousers are facing the wrong way, and my body was stuck and I got my head back the right way, and couldn't walk proper so I asked Lyn to pull my body back and I haven't taken my trousers off Mam, honest, she told me to and I didn't do it, she did it first anyway, because I was the doctor and I love you, Mam. And she made me do it.

There is a silence.

Dot   Go to bed.

John   Yes, Mam.

Doris   Oh, leave him.

Dot   Go to bed.

John   Aunty Doris?

Doris   Oh, Dot, leave him, he's told you the truth. He wants to stay up.

Dot   Bed.

John   Yes, Mam.

Edna   Aren't you going to say goodbye before you go?

John (*curtly*)   Goodbye. (*He turns to go.*)

Vic   Hey, come back here and say goodbye properly to your Aunty Edna; let her see you've got some manners.

John   Dad?

Vic   What?

John   Do I have to?

Edna   Come and give your Aunty Edna a kiss.

John   No.

Edna   Come on and give me a kiss, it's not that often that I see you. Come on, that's better, give your Aunty Edna a big kiss. (*She offers her cheek to* **John**.)

John *slowly approaches* **Edna** *and kisses her wincing as he does so.*

Edna   That's better.

Dot   Now go to bed . . .

John   Yes, Mam. Thanks. Don't hit me, will you?

Edna   Rebecca plays the clarinet, did I ever tell you? Is there any more tea, Dorothy?

John *exits.* **Edna** *freezes.*

Dot (*mocking*)   Is there any more tea?

Doris   What's got into you?

Dot   Her . . . their Edna. She makes me feel right awkward, as if I'm doing everything wrong. As if I'm on show all the time. . . . It's like meeting the Queen.

Vic   She's all right, she's like us. She started out just like us.

Edna   Rebecca speaks German, did I tell you?

Dot   But she makes me feel like we're thick or something. Does she think we're thick, Vic? Does she think *I'm* thick?

Vic   I don't know what she thinks, do I?

Doris   She doesn't like rich food, does she?

Edna   I'll get some fresh air.

Edna *exits.*

Dot   She thinks we're stupid.

Vic   Well, let's be honest, you do talk some rot.

Dot   Well, what have I got to talk to her about? And all that stuff about Rebecca. Rebecca this, Rebecca that. The poor kid hasn't got a life, she does everything that your Edna tells her. If he doesn't pass his eleven-plus I'll kill him, I will, I'll kill him. If he ever lets this family down I'll kill him.

Jack *enters the scene. It is nineteen sixty-seven.*

Doris   He failed, Dad.

Jack   It's him.

Vic   Who?

Jack   You. Your side. We've always had brains.

Liz   Who has?

Jack   We have.

Liz   I had the brains, Jack. I had the brains. You had the brawn. You've got the brawn, I've got the brains.

Jack   I've got brains, Liz.

Liz   But you never use them.

Doris   He should go to a special school.

Dot Doris?

Doris Well.

Vic He's not going down t' pit, whatever happens.

Doris They sent Christine Morgan to a special school. She never came back.

Vic So what? I'm not having my lad down a pit, Jack. I wouldn't wish that on a Jap.

Dot Stop shouting at our Doris.

Vic He's going to secondary modern and that's that. I'll have a word with him, we'll have a man-to-man. He can make his career working in a garage.

Jack He should be a prison warden.

Dot Dad?

Jack Prison warden.

Doris Bad company for a young lad, Dad.

Liz When he leaves school, a prison warden.

Jack A good job is that.

Vic Oh yeah, how do you know?

Jack Make a man of him that would. A prison warden.

Dot We've heard you.

Jack He can work wi' me at pit. I've got a shovel waiting for him.

Vic He'll do all right.

Doris You can visit when you want. Mrs Jackson's brother worked in a prison.

Vic I'll see to that.

Liz Vic's too soft with him.

Dot   You're too soft with him, and he's having no more comics.

Liz   He's been too soft, has Vic.

Vic   You buy him the comics. I bought him *Treasure Island* for Christmas and he never read it. He's not interested.

Doris   I never liked that.

Liz   What's that?

Doris   *Treasure Island.*

Liz   He'll find his own interests when he gets older.

Dot   Does anyone want any more tea?

Doris   There's a tart in the kitchen.

Vic   Is there?

Doris   There's a tart in the kitchen if anybody wants one; if anybody wants a tart, I've brought some, they're in the kitchen. They're lovely, I made them myself. Anybody want one?

There is a pause. Everyone looks at **Doris**.

All   No thanks.

Doris   They're nice!

The cast freezes. **John** *enters dressed as a twelve-year-old in nineteen sixty-eight.*

John (*to the audience*)   My Aunty Doris was an awful cook. A year later when I was at Clifton Secondary Modern she made a hundred Bakewell tarts and not one of them got eaten, and she still didn't get the message. I remember nineteen sixty-eight and the school at Clifton it certainly wasn't modern but it was definitely secondary.

The cast comes out of the freeze. **John** *is very distressed.*

Dot   What's wrong?

John   Nothing.

Liz   What's wrong?

Dot   There is.

Liz   What's the matter now?

Doris   Does he want a tart, I've brought some?

Vic   What's the matter?

John   Geek.

Vic   What?

John (*beginning to shake and cry*)   Geek . . .

Vic   Now listen, stop it, listen, listen; take a deep breath, calm down and tell me what's the matter.

John   Geek Davis keeps picking on me.

Dot (*hard*)   Well, pick on him back.

Vic   Don't encourage him to fight, Dot, let's bring him up right, shall we?

John   I can't.

Dot (*shouting*)   Why can't you?

Vic   Don't shout at him, he's upset.

Dot   I'm not shouting at him, Vic, I'm talking to him.

Doris   Look at him, he's all upset, he's a sensitive lad, aren't you? What's he upset for, what's happened?

Dot   Who is he, John, who is this Geek Davis?

Liz   What sort of a name is that?

John   He's a lad.

Vic   Is he an older lad?

John   Yeah.

Doris   I thought as much when he came in; I thought to myself, I bet an older lad's picking on him.

John   Every time ... I ... go out of the house, he comes and gets me.

Doris   How long has this been going on?

John   Since I went to Clifton.

Liz   He should never have gone to that school.

Doris   They should send him to a special school.

Liz   It's a disgrace, is that school.

Vic   And how long has he been picking on you?

John   Since the first day.

Vic   And have you ever done anything back?

John   No.

Dot   Right ... I'm going to see his mother. Where do they live?

John   I don't know, Mam.

Dot   You do. Where do they live, John?

John   I don't know.

Vic   Why? Why does he hit you?

Liz   What has he done to deserve being hit? Nothing. He's done nothing. They're picking on him for nothing.

John   He picks on me and he hits me and he shows me up.

Vic   Why, what does he do?

John   He pulls my ears when I'm in front of the girls and they all call me 'Big Ears'.

Liz (*kindly, softly*)   Oh, that's not nice.

John   And they all follow me around calling me 'Big Ears'.

Doris   He should never have had short hair.

Liz   Shut up, Doris.

Doris   Not with ears like that. He should never have had his hair cut short.

John   And he throws things at me, and spits on my coat.

Vic   How old is he?

John   Fifteen.

Dot   Where's he live?

Liz   Your grandad'll get him, won't you, Jack?

Jack (*bobbing and weaving, shadow-punching like a boxer*)   Jab him, John . . . when you see him, just jab him, no talking, right? Just a jab, and the old one-two. Hit first, ask questions second.

Dot   Don't, Dad.

Vic   We're trying to bring him up right.

Jack   Ar, and he's being picked on. Lad's scared to death.

Liz   Do you know them, Jack?

Doris   Who is it?

Liz   Davis.

Jack   I'll find out where they live, and I'll go around there and I'll smash every window in their bloody house.

Liz   Your grandad'll see to them.

Jack *is furious.*

Dot I don't want anybody picking on him. He's my son and I love him.

All the family is on tenterhooks.

Vic You love him too much; we've got to let him find his own way. Kids are cruel, they say all sorts. (*To* **John**.) Hey kid, listen to this. When I was as old as you, other lads used to call me 'Horse Teeth', they did. Because all my teeth had gone bad and I had to have false teeth. That was when I was as old as you.

Dot That's not true, Vic.

Vic It is. An' there was this lad, John, he had a nose that was so big, you know what the older lads used to call him?

John 'Big Nose.'

Vic No. 'Face.' They just called him 'Face', that's all; and you know what he does now?

John No.

Vic He's an insurance man.

Jack And he gets called a lot worse now than he ever did.

Vic If that's all what's happened we should leave it.

John That's not all.

Dot Why, what else is there?

John I can't tell you.

Vic John, we're your mam and dad, you can tell us anything.

Doris I knew there was something else. Nobody gets that worked up over being called 'Big Ears'.

Liz He hasn't got big ears, anyway, it's just that his hair is short.

John Today, when I was coming home from football practice with the Robins, he followed me.

Doris Who followed him?

Vic Geek Davis.

John I started to run. There was him, Fig, Jonah and some others who I didn't know, and some girls. I ran across the school field, but Geek caught up and dragged me down, and then they all caught up to us.

Vic And did you try and struggle?

John No.

Dot (*exasperated*) Our John . . .

John (*close to tears; it is very hard for him to tell his story*) And then . . . and then . . . two of them said did I know how to do the 'Three-Man-Lift', and I said 'No'. And then Geek said that this lad could pick up three people at once, and they said that they would show me. And they sat down one at each side, and all these girls came over and Geek said he was going to do the 'Three-Man-Lift', and these lads had hold of me at either side and I couldn't move and then they took my trousers down, and all the girls saw me . . . (*He bursts into tears.*) Mam . . . Mam . . . I wasn't doing anything to hurt them. Mam . . . Dad?

There is a silence.

Vic (*exploding*) Right, that's it! Where does he live? I'm having a word about this. Where does he live? Because I'm not having it, I'm not having that. I want a word about this, I'm not having my lad treated like that.

Jack Burn the lot of 'em.

Dot Look, just leave it.

Vic I'll . . . I'll . . . I'll smash every window in their bloody house and that's swearing, Jack, and you'll not often hear me swear.

Liz   They should leave him alone.

Vic   I will ... I'll swing for that Geek Davis or whatever his real name is.

Doris   Davis?

Vic   Geek Davis, Doris, are you deaf?

Doris   I was just thinking: Davis? I know that name. That must be Bud Davis's son. He went to school with me and our Dot. Oh, the whole family are a bunch of heathens. He's been in and out of prison more times than I've had hot dinners. Ken knows of 'em.

Dot   He was a bad 'un was Bud Davis.

Doris   I wun't meddle with them, Vic.

Liz   Your dad'll have 'em.

Dot   My dad's getting past that, Mam.

Doris   They once looked after a rabbit while somebody went on holiday, and by the time they'd got back Bud had skinned the rabbit and they'd had it in the pot.

Vic   I'm not bothered who they are, they have no right treating our John like that. It's not fair.

Jack *is still moving round the room, jabbing senselessly at the air. No one takes any notice of him.*

Jack   Hey John, remember, one-two, one-two. Jab, see, jab, jab.

Liz   He's a good lad; he loves his gran and that's all that matters.

Doris   He's got to stick up for himself though, Mam. He can't go through life like a drip.

Liz   He's a good lad, I don't want him fighting. I don't want him turning out like your dad.

Jack   What's wrong with me?

Liz   I don't want him being an animal like you.

Doris   Our Dot's too soft with him.

Dot   I'm not.

Liz   She's too soft with him is our Dorothy.

Vic   We want what's best for him, Jack; we don't want him to bring any trouble home but we don't want a drip.

Liz   She's too soft with him.

Dot   I'm not soft with him. (*To* **John**.) Come here, you, (*To* **Liz**.) I'll show you if I'm too soft with him.

Liz   Leave him, leave him, don't hit him.

Dot (*shaking* **John**)   I could hit you!

Rebecca *and* **Edna** *burst on the stage as if appearing in a musical.*

Edna   We've got some wonderful news, Vic, wonderful. Becky's been accepted at Cambridge. Isn't that fabulous? We're ever so pleased for her, we're taking her to Rome as a treat. Hope everything is fine with you. Come on, Rebecca.

Rebecca   Isn't it fantastic news? I'm sure you'll all be delighted.

Edna *and* **Rebecca** *exit. There is a silence.*

Dot   Go to bed.

John   Yes, Mam.

Dot   Come here . . .

John *moves to* **Dot**. *She hugs him.*

Dot   I love you kid. I love you. Now go to bed.

Doris *starts playing 'Happy Birthday' on a kazoo and picks up a briefcase wrapped in birthday paper. The others join in the singing and put on party hats secreted in the table.*

John   Dad, Dad, how does a sailor know there's a man in the moon?

Dot   We've heard it.

Vic   Our Doris hasn't.

John   Aunty Doris, how does a sailor know that there is a man in the moon?

Doris   I don't know. Is it because he's a sailor?

Vic   What?

John   No. It's because he's been to sea.

Jack   Useless.

John   Been to sea.

Dot   He should be on t' telly. He thinks he's funny.

Vic   Hey, that's a good joke that is. At least it's clean, not like what he usually comes out with.

John   It's because he's been to sea, Grandad.

Jack   I'm not thick.

Liz   Is he going to open it or what? Can he open it, Doris?

Doris   Course he can. Open your present. (*She hands the present to* **John**.)

Dot (*to* **Doris**)   You shouldn't bother. (*To* **Jack**.) Vic's been promoted, Dad.

Doris   I like to.

Dot (*to* **Doris**)   You've got no money. (*To* **Jack**.) Still at pit; Method Study.

Doris   We've saved up for it.

Dot (*to* **Doris**)   I know but . . . (*To* **Jack**.) He loves it.
No spade work now, eh?

Jack   Watching other men work. I wouldn't have
that.

Vic   It's good is that, been to sea. Our John's good at
jokes. Did you make it up?

John   I think so.

Jack   Method Study; men don't like 'em.

John *starts to tear the paper off the briefcase.*

Vic   That's a great joke that, I'll tell it at work. Make
it appear I've thought it up.

Dot   You needn't bother.

Jack   I wouldn't have a Method Study man telling
me what to do.

John *finishes unwrapping the briefcase, which looks very
expensive.*

Doris   I hope you like it.

John   It's great.

Liz   It's lovely that, isn't it? It's lovely.

Jack   What's he want an handbag for?

Liz   It's a briefcase.

Jack   I know.

John   It's great, Aunty Doris. Thanks, thanks a lot.

Doris   Give me a kiss. I'm not your Aunty Edna, I
won't bite.

John *kisses* **Doris**.

Dot (*inspecting the briefcase*)   Yes, it's just the job. I don't know if he's got anything worth putting in it, but it's just the job.

Doris It's for his schooling. I saw one in Skegness when we went away. I thought, I'll get our John one of them.

Vic Proper student now, kid?

Doris I was going to knit him another tank top, but then I thought, 'No, Doris, a change is as good as a rest.'

Liz (*producing a parcel*) And I've bought him a suit.

Doris Smashing.

Liz I saw it in the sale, fifteen pounds. Reduced from ninety-five. It's a bird's-eye pattern.

Dot Try it on for your Aunty Doris.

John Mam?

Dot Try it on.

Liz Leave him. He looks smart in it, Doris. Just right for school.

John I'm not wearing it for school, am I?

Dot Course you are.

John (*to the audience*) I looked like one of the Royal Family in it.

Liz It suits you, you don't want to be like all the others.

John (*to the audience*) I looked like an old man in it.

Doris How's he doing at school?

Vic He's doing all right. We've had his Options meeting to pick his subjects.

Dot He said he wanted to be an actor.

Vic   He just came out with it. I didn't know where to put myself.

Jack   A bloody actor?

Vic   He said he wanted to be an actor or a doctor. So they've got him doing Drama and Chemistry. When we got out of that office I could have gone mad with him. I've spent the last nine months convincing him he isn't going to play football for Leeds.

Liz   I want him to be a doctor, then if ever there's anything wrong with me our John'll be able to look after me. I don't like going to t' doctors.

Jack   Is he still playing for t' Robins?

Vic   He scored four on Sat'day.

Jack   Ar.

Dot   He's a clown is our John, you have to watch him.

John (*to the audience*)   I was with that haircut.

Dot   He's a clown, takes after Vic.

Vic   I'm educating him, Jack. I give him a new word every time I get the *Reader's Digest: Increase Your Word Power*. There's power in words, Jack.

John (*to the family*)   My dad's favourite word at the moment is axiomatic.

Doris   Oh heck.

Jack   I'll trim them hedges if you want, Vic?

Liz   Get wrapped up if you're going out.

Vic   You can leave it, you know, Jack. I can do it.

Dot   Just sit down, Dad, relax.

Liz   He looks smart in that suit Doris, he does.

Doris   He should get himself a little job.

Vic   He's got a paper round.

John   I've got myself a job, helping my mother clean up. It's a full-time job. School work is just part-time.

Jack   Get a job, then he'll know what work is.

John   I know what work is.

Vic   Aye, he could watch it all day.

John   Anyway, I might leave home and go and live with my gran, eh, Gran?

Dot   She doesn't want you. She only wants you because she knows you have to go home.

Liz   He can stop when he likes but I'm getting too old now.

John   No you're not, you're only twenty-one really.

Liz   I wish I was.

Jack   She does too much.

Liz   Don't start.

John   So that's where it comes from, I thought you didn't overdo it?

Liz   Well, his grandad's like a cat on hot bricks, he can't keep still.

Jack   She should be taking it steady.

Vic   She likes to keep active, don't you, Ma?

Liz   Well, what am I supposed to do, sit and watch the goldfish all day? I'd end up like our Doris's Ken.

Doris   Mother. It's a birthday.

Jack   Now, now, you two.

Liz   Well, he's such a funny man. We don't ever see

your Uncle Ken, John.

Jack   Not on a birthday, Liz.

Dot   Leave it, Mam.

Liz   I mean is he still alive, or is he dead, or has he left her, or what?

Jack   When're you getting a new car then, Vic?

Vic   Get one next year, Pa, all being well.

Doris *is very tender on the subject of Ken; nervously she can't resist rising to the bait.*

Doris   He stays in, he never goes out. We live our own life and we're happy and that's the end of it.

Liz   I don't think I've seen him twice since they were married.

Vic   Yeah, he's not been out since he lost his teeth in the sea at Torquay.

Doris   Don't exaggerate, Mother.

Vic   He lost his teeth, isn't that right, Doris? (*To* **John**.) Your Uncle Ken lost his teeth in the sea on the first day of their honeymoon and they didn't speak to each other for the rest of the week.

Doris   I don't think it's funny, Vic.

Vic   And apparently his suck was worse than his bite.

Dot (*sharply*)   Stop it!

Doris   It wasn't Torquay, it was Yarmouth. And in any case I've got my dogs; Ken stays in and I look after the dogs. I know he's funny, but we're happy and I don't think there's any reason for Vic to make him a laughing stock. And after I've bought our John that present I don't expect to come here and get humiliated. That cost us thirty-five pounds, that briefcase.

Jack You'll set her off, you know what she's like.

Doris And I don't thank you, Mother, for bringing it up.

Liz (*as if she's played no part*) I've said nothing.

Doris (*close to tears*) I'm not having it.

John Aunty Doris.

Doris I'm going. I'm not stopping here, I'm going. (*She stands, in tears.*)

Dot Oh nip, sit down.

Doris I'm not . . . I'm going, it's not fair. I can't make him come out of the house, I can't tell him what to do; do you think I don't want him to come home? It was my dad – my dad said some awful things when we got married.

Liz Your dad never wanted you to marry Ken!

Doris My Dad said some awful things and Ken said he'd never forgive him and he hasn't done. And my dad won't take it back and Ken won't take it back.

Jack I'm not taking anything back, he's still a snake as far as I'm concerned.

Dot It was Vic that started all this.

Vic I was only having a laugh, telling the tale.

Doris Well, it wasn't funny.

Liz She's highly strung is our Doris, she always has been.

Dot (*to* **Liz**, *shouting*) You set her off.

Liz Who are you shouting at?

Doris Well, I'm glad your opinion of Ken's never changed, Dad, because it wouldn't be like you to change your opinion. Me and Ken are happy enough and I'll tell you this, I'll never come up here again as long as I live.

Doris *exits in tears. There is a silence.* **Doris** *returns, still crying.*

Doris   Forgot me knitting bag.

The others laugh, kindly. Mantovani's 'The Way You Look Tonight' softly fades in. **John** *and* **Doris** *exit.* **Liz**, **Jack**, **Dot** *and* **Vic** *enter as if returning from the theatre. During the following, they remove their party hats.*

Liz   Oh, wasn't it fantastic?

Vic   Lovely, wasn't it?

Liz   One of the best nights in years. I'll never forget it, I never will. Come on, Jack, let's dance.

Jack   No.

Liz   Come on.

Jack   I don't want.

Liz   Oh, you spoilsport.

Vic   Come on, Ma, I'll dance with you.

Dot   Look at me mam.

Vic *and* **Liz** *dance slowly to the music.*

Liz   Go steady, Vic, you're all over my feet.

Vic   Sorry, Ma.

Dot   Vic can't do anything right for me mam.

Liz   He's better than your dad, he used to cripple me.

Jack   I'm better than Vic at everything.

Dot   Where is he?

Liz   He's trying on his costume again for me, I

thought it was beautiful.

Dot (*calling off*)   Come on Errol Flynn, we're all waiting.

Liz   I'll have to sit down, Vic, I feel a bit dizzy. I'm not as nippy as I thought I was.

Vic   Do you want to dance, Pa?

Jack   Get away, you daft sod.

Liz   Fantastic. It was a beautiful evening.

Dot   Well, I've got to say, I was proud of him. I couldn't see out of my eyes for crying.

John *enters. He is dressed as a lion and growling.*

Vic   Look out, King of the Jungle's here.

Liz   Well, he looks even better close up. He was the best thing in it. There was only one problem: he wasn't on long enough. Why didn't you have a bigger part?

Vic   It's his first year in the Youth Theatre, Ma.

Liz   Well, you look a million dollars.

Dot (*to* **Liz** *slightly anxiously*)   Are you all right, Mam?

Liz   I'm all right.

Dot   You look a bit pale.

Liz   It's the weather. I don't like warm weather. I like it when it's cold, put a bit of colour in my cheeks. Eh, John. Eh? Put a bit of colour in your gran's cheeks.

Vic   He's French, the playwright, Mam.

Liz (*revelling in the recent memory*)   Oh, but he was good.

Vic   Yeah, next year they might give him a speaking part.

Jack   Ar. He wasn't on long.

Liz He was fantastic, he was the best lion I've seen.

Vic . I can remember him at the junior school. He was in *Sleeping Beauty*. He was a tree. He was the only tree that picked his nose.

Dot We know that, you couldn't contain yourself. Every time he came on you started clapping.

Vic Well, I'm proud of him. Hey, can you remember when he was in the Nativity?

Dot Not again, Vic. (*To* **Liz**.) Are you sure you're all right, Mam?

Liz I'm fine.

Vic (*loudly*) 'Is there a baby here, the stars are shining so brightly.'

Dot Vic, why are you telling me this? I was there.

Vic He shouted that loud you could hear him in the Post Office next door.

Liz He was a good shepherd.

John Did you enjoy it, Grandad?

Jack Well.

Liz It's not your grandad's thing. He's more for sport and horse racing, aren't you?

Jack (*reluctantly*) I didn't like it.

Liz Jack.

Jack Well, I didn't, no use pretending. All that way to Rotherham and he wasn't on two minutes.

John I'll go and take my costume off.

John *slowly exits.*

Dot Dad, be a bit sensitive.

Jack I thought it was a load of rubbish. I couldn't

understand it, for a start.

Liz Well, you shouldn't have come, then.

Jack I didn't want to in the first place. That's the trouble with this family; nobody says what they really think.

Vic Lad's interested in acting, Pa.

Vic *exits.*

Jack It's a woman's job. A nancy's job.

Liz Don't be so crude, Jack.

Jack I'm only saying.

Liz Everybody's not like you, you know; other people have feelings.

Jack It'd be better if more people were like me, you wouldn't put up with such shit. To be honest, it wasn't my cuppa tea, in fact after our John had been on I was ready for home. And a lot of others were and all.

Dot Sometimes, Dad . . .

John *enters, dressed as a fourteen-year-old. He watches the scene.*

Jack Always tell the truth, no matter about hurting people. Always tell the truth. He knows his grandad does.

Dot Yeah, even if it's crippling.

Dot *exits.*

Liz Well, I thought he was fantastic.

Liz *exits.*

Jack Well, I didn't and that's that. He's not bothered anyway, lad's not bothered. He's gunna face a lot worse than that. (*To* **John**.) He's not bothered, are you . . . ?

Jack *freezes.* **John** *comes forward. The rest of the cast moves into the background.*

John (*to the audience*)   My grandad didn't like me being in plays. And when I started playing rugby he got really confused.

Rebecca *enters. It is early nineteen seventy-two;* **Rebecca** *is a student at Cambridge and dresses accordingly.*

Rebecca   Mummy's in the garden with Uncle Vic. Your garden is so small, I never realised before. You're so close to your neighbours, it's awful; it's not very private, is it? It's ever so warm out there; it's a sun-trap.

John   Yeah.

Rebecca   Good weather for a study break.

John   Yeah.

Rebecca   I was going to play Uncle Vic something on the clarinet but you can't hear for the dogs.

John   Might sound a lot better.

Rebecca   Uncle Vic is so funny.

John   Start a new trend, dog and wind instrument?

Rebecca   He's really good at jokes. I'm awful.

John   Really?

Rebecca   I think your grandfather is teasing the dogs.

John   Oh, right.

Rebecca   He seems to have a way with dogs.

John   He's been surrounded by them all his life.

Rebecca   Yes, Uncle Vic is very good at jokes.

John   Yeah.

Rebecca   Yes. He said he'd like to hear me play.

Another time, maybe.

John   Yes, he likes Acker Bilk.

Rebecca   Really?

There is a silence.

What sort of things are you doing at the moment?

John   All sorts.

Rebecca   I suppose you'll be thinking about jobs soon. Would you like to work at the pit?

John   No. I'd like to stay at school.

Rebecca   Is there much homework?

John   A bit.

There is a silence.

Rebecca (*working hard to keep the conversation going*)   I sent you a card from Paris; did you get it?

John   No.

Rebecca   Oh, well, I did send one. We went to Paris, and then we went to Rome. I'd been before but we went with some friends from college.

John   Oh.

Rebecca   You should see Rome, it's fascinating.

John   Is it?

Rebecca   I went with Mum before I went down. Almost everywhere you look there are these incredibly old buildings, and monuments, and fountains. It really is fantastic. And the fact that that is the centre, you know, the centre of all this civilisation. You'd love it.

John   Yeah?

Rebecca   You should go.

John Why?

Rebecca Because you'd enjoy it.

John Oh.

Rebecca Have you been to Europe?

John No.

There is a silence. **Edna** *enters.*

Edna Oh, it's so warm. I think the dogs are sweating. I could certainly smell something out there and I'm sure it wasn't human.

Rebecca I was just telling John about Rome.

Edna Oh, really.

Rebecca He said he hasn't been abroad.

Edna What, not even to Wales?

John No.

Edna What about your mum and dad?

John Not as far as I know.

Edna Really. I thought Vic had been to Scotland during National Service?

John Dunno.

Edna Beautifully clean, isn't it, Rebecca? The house!

There is a slight pause.

Rebecca Well you must go, John, because it's unbelievable.

Edna (*answering herself*) Beautifully clean.

John I do most of it.

Rebecca Mother doesn't bother much.

John On my hands and knees.

Edna   I wonder if Aunt Dorothy is making any tea,
Rebecca? Do you have Rington's, John?

John   I don't want to go abroad because I've heard
that it smells.

Edna   Rome? No. Venice, slightly in summer.

John   And the food's not very good. No, we have
Typhoo.

Rebecca   Where did you hear that?

John   I read it in a book.

Rebecca   You read it then, you didn't hear it.

Edna   Don't believe everything you read, John. Just
because something's in a book, doesn't mean that it's
entirely true.

Rebecca   You should see for yourself. Don't believe
others.

John   Why should I believe you, then?

Edna   Because why should we lie to you?

John   Why should anyone lie in a book?

Edna   It's not a lie, darling. It's a different opinion.
Do you think we could have tea?

Rebecca   I think it's amazing. I'd never thought
about it before. You're, what are you now?

John   Nearly fifteen.

Rebecca   And you've never been out of the country.

John   I'm not interested.

Rebecca   Don't you want to see the world?

John   No. I've never been anywhere except Blackpool.

Rebecca   Blackpool?

John   Yeah, we go there on holiday, and we all sleep in one bed, and we have a potty underneath the bed just in case. Have you ever been?

Rebecca   No, actually, I haven't.

John   You should go, it's absolutely unbelievable.

Alma Cogan singing 'Hernando's Hideaway' plays. **Edna** *and* **Rebecca** *exit. The lights change, coming up on* **Jack**, **Doris**, **Vic**, **John**, **Liz** *and* **Dot**. *They are arranged around the table in a tableau that indicates that they are faced with a problem; the scene is reminiscent of pictures of Mafia families. The costumes and lighting are fairly monochromatic, with nothing garish on stage. The music fades. There is silence, broken only by the sounds of a dog barking occasionally off, and the fidgeting of the family.*

Vic   Go on.

John   Someone broke my nose.

Vic   Who?

John   Dad, why?

Vic   Who was it?

John   It's not important.

Dot   We want to know who it is, we want to know what you were doing for somebody to break your nose.

John   Why can't we just leave it and get our dinners?

Liz   Because nobody is hungry.

John   I am.

Vic   We want to know what happened.

John (*sighing*)   OK, I was coming back from the cinema –

Dot   He's always at the bloody pictures. Him and Tub are always at the pictures.

Vic   Let him tell the tale.

Doris   What film was it?

John   *Zulu.*

Dot   It wasn't, so don't lie.

John   It was *Zulu.*

Dot   It was *Twins of Evil*, because I checked in the paper.

Vic   So you shouldn't have been there in the first place.

Dot   It was an X certificate.

Doris   Disgusting, that.

Dot   I'm ashamed of him.

John   What have I done wrong? Everyone in the school goes.

Liz   I've never liked that school.

Vic   And we know about your books.

John (*shocked*)   Books?

Vic   Books.

John   What books?

Vic   What books, what books! We weren't born yesterday. Don't give us that. Do I have to spell it out for you?

John (*innocently*)   Yeah, I don't know what books you mean.

Vic   I mean those books which you keep in the record cabinet. That you'd thought you'd hide from us, that you thought we wouldn't find, those books inside the record sleeves.

John   Oh, yeah.

Vic   You should have known your mother would find them, she cleans everywhere.

Doris   That's disgusting, I think.

John   They're not my books, anyway, they're Tub's.

Dot   Well, you'd better give them back to him in that case, because I don't want them in this house. In fact I'll tell his mother when I see her and she can come around and collect them.

John   I don't think he wants them back.

Dot   No, I thought she might-not.

John   So they can go in the dustbin. I was going to throw them away myself, but I've been busy doing the housework.

Dot   Right, Vic, them books – dustbin, I don't want to see them.

John   I never looked at them anyway. I'm not interested in that sort of stuff.

Vic   Well, you've got quite a little collection for somebody who's not interested in them. I counted over twenty.

Dot (*to* **Vic**)   What were you doing with them?

Vic   Counting them.

John   Well, I hope you've put them all back because they're his dad's.

Vic   They're going in the bin and don't try and avoid the issue: get on with the story.

John   You brought it up.

Liz   Will that chicken be ready, Dot?

Dot   It can wait, Mam.

John   Anyway I came out of the cinema, and it's

been a good night, not brilliant. The film was crap.

Dot *clips* **John**.

Dot   Language at the table.

John   Sorry.

Vic   Get on with it.

Dot   He dramatises everything.

John   So I walk home and these two figures are standing at the top of the hill; I can't see who they are. They stop me and ask me for a chip.

Liz   You should keep off chips.

Dot   He doesn't have them in this house.

John   And the next thing I know there's blood all over my shirt, my nose feels numb and he's hit me.

Vic   Who?

John   Geek Davis.

Liz (*as angry as her mild manner allows*)   Oh, that lad.

Doris   The family are a nuisance.

Vic   And what did you do?

John   What could I do?

Dot   You could have hit him back.

John   I had a bag full of chips.

Vic   That's no excuse.

John   What did you want me to do, chip him to death?

Liz   You should've stuck up for yourself.

John   Gran?

Liz   You should.

John   I didn't know he was going to hit me. It was pitch black. What do you think he had, a big sign saying 'Look out, the end is nigh'?

Jack (*slowly; deadly serious*)   It's about time you did something about it, because if you don't, I'm warning you he'll make the rest of your life a misery. While ever our John's around here he'll make his life a misery. Now this is thee grandad telling you. Fight back.

There is a silence.

John   I don't want to.

Jack (*shocked*)   You don't want to?

John   No.

Jack (*shouting*)   What are you going to do?

Liz   Jack, stop shouting.

Jack   He'll let everybody in the world shit on him.

Liz   Now Jack, that's gone far enough.

John   Well, me mam shits on me dad.

Dot   Dad, don't get worked up.

Jack   Well, it's about time somebody said something about our John because Vic's too lily-livered to do anything about it.

Liz   Now don't start.

Vic   What do you mean by that?

Liz   Jack, you've upset one, don't upset another.

Jack   You know what I mean.

Liz   He'll lose a friend in Vic if he starts.

Jack   Somebody has to say it.

Liz   Take no notice of him, Vic, he doesn't mean

what he says.

Vic   Our lad's been hit, Jack, now I say forget it.

Jack   Forget it. He's like a nancy.

John   Who is?

Dot   Shut up, you.

John   I'm not like a nancy.

Liz   Shut up.

John   Gran?

Doris   Dad, stop shouting. We can have a rational conversation. Just stop shouting or you'll make yourself bad.

Vic   (*beginning to lose his temper*)   I'm warning you, Jack, don't say what you're thinking, because it's not fair. Now I'm warning you. This is my house. I pay the rent here.

Doris   You should have bought this house.

Jack   You're warning me.

Vic   I am.

Jack   (*tense*)   You're warning me?

Vic   I am, yes.

Jack   You.

Doris   You should have bought this house when we bought ours.

Vic   Yes, me.

Jack   You're warning me. I've eaten bigger men than you.

Dot   Oh, for God's sake, Dad.

Liz   Jack.

Dot   Dad.

Liz   Vic, forget it, forget it. He goes off the deep end and he doesn't know what he's saying.

The atmosphere is tense. **Jack** *and* **Vic** *are straining to get at each other, but of course both realise the consequences.*

Jack   I've beaten men like you with double bronchitis. In fact I'll have you now . . . come on, come on here. I'll have you now. (*He gets up.*) Come on.

Liz   Jack.

Doris   You're making my mam bad.

Vic (*standing*)   Get out of my house.

Dot   Oh.

Vic   Get out.

Jack   You're warning me?

Vic   Get out.

John   You're both crackers.

Vic   Get out Jack, I'm not having it.

Jack   You will have it if you come here. You'll have it on the nose end.

Vic   And now I'm telling you.

Jack   You're telling me?

Vic   I'm not warning you, I'm telling you. Get out of this house and don't ever come back again.

Dot   Now stop it, stop it, the pair of you. Stop it.

Liz   Vic, he doesn't mean it, do you Jack? Vic, Vic, he doesn't mean it.

Doris   Dad, calm down.

Jack   I mean it. I bloody well mean it.

Vic Get out!

Jack (*appealing to* **Liz**) I'm not having him talk to me like that. I didn't have men at the pit talk to me like that. I'm not having some trump Time-and-Motion man talk to me like that.

Vic Why, who are you?

Liz Think of our John. Jack, it's no good him seeing all this, think of the lad. Jack, I'm pleading with you, please, please . . . I'm pleading with you. (*She is extremely upset and begins to cough.*)

Doris Dad, just pack it in.

Jack I'm not being shouted at like that.

John Oh no.

Dot (*to* **John**, *exploding with rage*) You shut up you, shut up. Otherwise I'll hit you and it won't be like Geek Davis, it'll be a real smack and I'll knock some sense into your head. Watching dirty films, you're pathetic.

Liz Leave him, Dorothy.

John It's like a madhouse.

Vic You've heard your mother, and she's told you to shut up. If you'd got any guts at all we wouldn't be arguing. Why didn't you hit him back, why didn't you run off, are you that thick? For goodness' sake, you're living in a dream world.

Dot All his life is a bloody play.

Vic We must be the laughing-stock in the Davis house.

Jack He lives in a Walter Mitty world.

Doris He does.

Dot He's only interested in one thing.

John I'm not.

Dot Making people laugh; well, they're laughing all right. They're laughing right in your face.

John This family? I've got a broken nose and nobody's bothered about that.

Liz What did he hit you for?

Dot He was probably playing the fool. Doing one of those silly walks or whatever he does.

Doris He needs to grow up. He's too highly strung.

John Listen who's talking.

Vic Stop your back-chat, you, my lad.

Jack I've pulled this family up by the boot straps. . . . I had nothing, nothing. I've had to fight for every little bit of respect.

Vic (*exasperated*) I don't know what we're going to make of him. Why didn't you have a go back at them?

John Because I'm scared.

Jack Scared?

Doris You're scared?

Dot What are you scared of?

John Being hurt.

Vic (*lost*) I don't know.

John What can I do against Geek Davis? All the kids on the estate are scared of him. He's a right maniac, he's an amateur boxer or something. He just hit me for a laugh. He thinks I'm soft.

Liz You are.

There is a silence.

Vic (*lost*) I don't know.

Dot   Right. He can stay in this house for a month.

There are winces of approval and nods of satisfaction from the family.

John   A month?

Dot   A month.

John   That's my mother's answer to everything, she should have been a judge.

Vic   No more dirty books, no more sneaking off to the pictures in a dirty mac. I'll put a stop to that, he can stay in and help me. My car's playing me up, he can help me with that, it's about time he learned to do something technical. I'll show him who's boss in this house. I want to keep my eye on him.

Jack   He should take up boxing.

Dot   Dad, you've said enough now.

Jack   Boxing. One two. Don't ask questions. Bang. (*He throws a short stabbing right.*) Bang.

Doris   He can help Ken clean his garage out, Vic, if you want him to do some dirty work, as a punishment, you know?

Jack   I want to know if we've got a man in the family. I want to know what he's going to do about it? He's farting about in bloody plays.

Dot   Dad, please. Honestly. Please. Can we leave it now?

John   There's not a lot I can do, is there? I'm being locked up for a month.

Liz   He wants one of them things out of the catalogue. They're in our Doris's catalogue.

Doris   I don't know what you're on about.

Liz   Is it a 'Cow-worker'? Get him one of them. How

to kick sand in somebody's face in ten seconds a day. (*To* **Dot**.) Don't you feed him?

Dot   Course we feed him.

Liz   What on, sausage meat?

Dot   Mother, we feed him.

Liz   He needs fish.

Dot   He gets fish.

Liz   What sort of fish?

Dot   Fish fish.

Liz   He needs fresh fish.

Jack   He needs milk, meat and fish.

Vic   He needs vegetables.

Doris   He needs calcium.

Liz   He needs chicken and vitamins.

Jack   He needs his body building up, he's like a piece of bloody string.

Doris   I bet that chicken'll be burnt.

Dot   And it's all his silly fault.

John   You'd better put another month on my sentence.

Dot   Don't be so clever you, you're not too old to get a good hiding.

John   I've just had a good hiding.

Liz   He needs fish.

Doris   I can smell burning.

Dot   That bloody chicken.

Music plays. All rush off except **John**. *The music fades.*

John (*to the audience*)   My Aunty Doris was right: the chicken was burnt; so were the spuds, the cabbage, the peas and the gravy. And it was the only Sunday dinner I can remember that consisted solely of Arctic Roll. When my 'Bullworker' arrived from the catalogue it was so tightly wrapped and I was so weak that I couldn't get it out of the wrapper. So we sent it back to Kays. But it didn't matter anyway, because my Uncle Ken had some weights in his garage and he said that I could have them. So I started weight training. My dad, in an effort to show off his manhood, got tennis elbow from over-straining with the weights and was off work for three weeks.

The lights change. It is almost a year later. **Vic** *enters; he is clearly very happy.*

Vic   Ha ha ... I knew it ... I knew it ... I knew he wouldn't let us down. Ha ha ... fantastic.... Oh, wait till I tell our Edna he's done as well as Rebecca.

Dot *enters. She looks at* **Vic**.

Dot   She's got ten O levels. . . .

Vic   I'm going to watch *Calendar*, then I'll go and I'm going to phone our Edna. Nine CSE grade ones.

Dot   They're better aren't they?

Vic   I knew it, I did, I could feel it in my water. And he said he didn't even try. I knew he would do it. Jarring Jack Jackson.

Dot   You're alway over the top, like your Edna. Calm down, your false teeth are slipping.

Vic   I'm pleased.

Dot   I knew he'd do it.

Vic   Yeah?

Dot   Of course, it was axiomatic.

Vic (*to* **John**)   Come here, you.

John   Don't, Dad.

Vic   Let me give you a kiss. (*He kisses* **John**.)

Dot   Look at your dad, he'll burst a blood vessel. He's as soft as a brush. He's crying.

Vic   Course I'm crying.

Dot   You're always over the top. He gets carried away. He's mentally unstable is your dad.

Vic   What are you going to do with your qualifications, kid?

John   I think I'd like to be a prison warden.

Vic (*to* **Dot**)   Come here, you.

Diane Washington singing 'September in the Rain' plays. **Vic** *grabs* **Dot** *and they dance. The lights change – perhaps a mirror-ball effect can be used – to show how transported they are.* **John**, *watching his parents dance, is picked out by a spotlight.*

John (*to the audience*)   There was a great celebration in our house the night I got my CSE results. And from then on I could hold my head up on the bus with the lads who went to grammar school. That night my dad had half a lager and my mother had a brandy. They really went to town. And I had my own celebration. I went out, drank a full bottle of Pernod, kissed Lyn Sutton full on the lips, took her to a disco and returned home at half-one drunk as a skunk. My dad was furious but could understand my feelings. My mother, characteristically, said nothing. She simply hit me in the face with a shoe.

He exits. The lights change to green, to indicate that we are now in the garden. It is nineteen seventy-three. **Liz**, **Rebecca**, **Dot**, **Jack**, **Edna** *and* **Vic** *are onstage, sitting in garden chairs.* **Liz** *looks very ill and has a blanket tucked around her;*

Dot *and* **Doris** *sit looking at her.* **Jack** *contemplates the sky.* **Vic** *looks warm and contented. There are the faint sounds of birdsong and dogs barking.* **Dot** *gets up and tucks the blanket around* **Liz**.

Dot   Are you warm enough, Mam?

Liz   Warm enough? I'm roasting.

Dot (*louder*)   Are you warm enough?

Liz   Stop fussing.

Doris   Is she warm enough?

Dot   She's all right now.

Liz   You'd think I was a new-born baby with this treatment.

Doris   Tuck her in.

Edna   That looks better.

Liz   Look at me. I'm like an old woman.

Vic   You'll be all right, Ma, Dot'll see to you.

Jack   I told her she'd overdo it. She's cleaning all the time. She still thinks she's in service.

Liz (*easily*)   Shut up, you.

Jack   She's made herself bad.

Liz   Oh, he's off again.

Jack   I'm only telling the truth.

Doris   She's warm enough.

John *enters; his lip is slightly bruised.*

John   Are you all right, Gran?

Liz   I'm smashing, kid. Never felt better. All this fuss over nothing. Your mother. She panics. Have you hurt your lip?

John   Messing with them weights.

Vic   We're a family of panickers, Ma. I panic at the least little thing.

Liz   He's got a bruised lip.

John   It's you I'm more bothered about.

Liz (*matter-of-fact*)   I don't know how this family'll go on when there's a bereavement. You've all got faces as long as a wet week and I'm not even dead yet.

Doris   Mam?

Liz   Well, we'll not be here for ever, will we, Pa?

Jack (*quietly*)   Speak for yourself.

Liz   He thinks he's Peter Pan, does your dad.

They all laugh uncomfortably.

Doris   You'll outlive us, you, I don't know what you're talking about.

Edna   Don't get a chill, you know, Grandma.

Dot   Do you want another sandwich, Edna? There's plenty left.

Doris   Go on, get one, help yourself.

Dot   There's plenty left.

Vic   There's hundreds left. She always makes too many. You'd think she was feeding the whole estate.

Doris   There's a tart if she wants one. I've made them with that wholemeal flour.

Edna   No thanks.

Doris   Rebecca?

Rebecca   Yes, I'll have one, they sound nice.

Jack (*quietly*)   She's risking her life having one of them tarts.

Doris Oh, somebody wants one of my tarts. (*She moves to the exit.*) Put the flag out.

Vic Phone the papers, Doris.

Doris *exits.*

Dot John, you'd better phone for an ambulance.

John (*looking at* **Liz** *as if worried about her*) Why?

Dot Rebecca'll need one.

John (*relieved*) It must be Christmas, my mother made a joke.

Liz Our Doris is pleased with herself, isn't she?

Vic She's about to commit an act of genocide, Ma.

John *Reader's Digest* again?

Vic You can't beat it.

John It's unbeatable

Vic Of course it is.

Dot She's had twins, Mam.

Liz Who, our Doris? I thought they weren't having any.

John }
Vic } (*half-hearing the other conversation; together*) Eh?
What?

Dot The dogs have had twins.

Liz Nobody told me.

Dot We did.

Jack She's forgot.

Liz I haven't forgot; nobody told me.

Vic   Tina and Trixie.

Jack (*in disbelief*)   Our Doris, tut tut tut tut . . .

Vic   Tina and Trixie?

Liz   Lovely names.

Doris *returns with a large tray of tarts.*

Doris   Here we are. The feeding of the five thousand.

Liz   You didn't tell me, did you?

Doris   Tell you what?

Liz   About the dogs.

Doris   No, I haven't told you.

Liz   See.

Doris   Our Dot told you.

Liz   But I knew you hadn't told me. They think I'm going senile.

Vic   We don't.

Doris   Here you are Rebecca, take your pick. (*She presents the tarts to* **Rebecca**.)

Rebecca   Doesn't anyone else . . . ?

Jack   We've had them before.

Rebecca *takes a tart and tastes it.*

Liz   . . . think I'm going senile.

Rebecca   Actually they're quite nice.

John   Wait till they've settled in your stomach . . . you'll not be able to move. They're like concrete.

Doris   Hey, you, don't be so cheeky.

Doris *exits.*

John Only joking.

Vic So what's new, Rebecca?

Rebecca (*still chewing*) They're quite nice.

Vic Did you know she's got a first class degree, kid? That's fantastic.

Dot I've brought some wine special, Edna. Blue Nun. Do you like it?

Doris *enters.*

Doris Isn't it warm? Close, isn't it?

Dot Does anybody want any wine?

Liz What, she got a first what?

Edna Not for me Dorothy, really.

John She's passed her exams.

Dot More tea then, anybody? Any more for any more?

Vic Sit down, relax, get some sun on you.

Liz She's as white as a sheet, is our Dot.

Doris Look who's talking.

Edna We think she's going to stay on. She's been offered a research place.

Jack That sun's warm . . .

Edna I think she'll probably stay in Cambridge.

Jack It's a sun-trap, this garden. I always said it was.

Rebecca Mum wants to sort all the things out for me, Uncle Vic.

Jack A really nice quiet piece of God's earth this is.

Rebecca She thinks she's living my life for me.

Edna I don't, dear, I only want what's for the best.

Rebecca The best for who, Mother?

Doris How's that tart gone down?

Rebecca Fine.

Doris Do you want another?

Jack She's trying to kill her.

Vic First class honours, that's fantastic, eh, kid?

Rebecca I'm not living my life for my mother, not any more.

Edna (*tensely*) Rebecca . . .

Vic Do you still play the clarinet?

Rebecca On and off.

Edna She's very good, Vic, she's Grade Eight. But she's lazy. She needs pushing.

Rebecca I want to travel. I fancy working in India.

Dot India? I've got some place-mats made in India. Got pictures of the Taj Mahal on them.

Rebecca Oh really?

Dot They're lovely.

Rebecca I want to see as much of the world as I can. Mummy would rather I was shut away.

Vic University of Life, eh, Rebecca?

Dot (*to* **John**) Go and get them place-mats from India, show Rebecca.

John She dun't want to see 'em.

Vic Are we ever going to hear you play, Rebecca?

Dot Vic, don't, it's not fair.

Rebecca   I haven't got my clarinet.

Edna   You have dear, it's in the car.

Vic   Be nice that, nice bit of music, eh, kid?

Doris   She's not going to play, is she?

Vic   Be lovely that.

Edna   When she's travelled I think she'll go back to university. She just has to get this wanderlust out of her system.

Liz   You never told me you'd had twins, Doris.

Dot   I told you.

Liz   Just feel me, will you; am I cold?

Doris and **Edna** *dash over to* **Liz**.

Doris (*touching* **Liz**)   No, you're smashing, you daft old brush.

Rebecca   Is she all right?

Doris   She's smashing.

Rebecca   I'm never going back, Mum, you go back if you're so keen. I'm up to here with it. (*She pauses.*) I'll go to the car.

Rebecca *exits*.

Edna   So what about John? What's next after A levels?

Vic   He's just been in another play, Edna: *Dark of the Moon*.

Liz   I want him to be a doctor.

Edna   Has he thought about teaching, Vic? Has he ever thought about being a teacher? Very few people make it in creative professions, you know, Vic. It's something to fall back on. . . .

Dot Just at the moment, Edna, he's into this weight-lifting lark. But it won't last, it never does, and you can't keep him away from the cinema.

Edna Rebecca has no interest in the cinema.

Doris She's not going to play sommat classical is she?

Edna That sun is so hot.

Dot Vic, go and get that sun hat from Blackpool for your Edna. It says 'Kiss Me Quick' on it, Edna. You'll be all right with that.

Edna I think I'll just stand in the shade. (*She moves to stand in the shade.*)

Jack Beautiful garden.

Dot If ever I'm feeling a bit low, I sit at the window and look out into my garden.

Vic That's when she's finished cleaning up.

Dot Shut up, Horse Teeth.

Vic Come here, give us a cuddle.

Dot What for?

Vic Because I hate you, what do you think?

Liz (*jokingly*) Oh Vic, steady on.

Vic Do you want a cuddle as well, Ma?

Vic *cuddles* **Dot***, simply and not sloppily; they are clearly in love.*

Jack (*to* **John**) Still playing rugby?

John Ar.

Jack Still doing plays?

John Ar.

Jack How's weights going?

John Allrate.

There is a silence.

Jack Let's have a feel at your arms.

John No, get away.

Liz Come here, I'll have a feel. (*She feels* **John***'s arms, then moves a hand to his head and ruffles his hair.*) Oh yeah, lovely, that is.

John Don't say it, Dad.

Vic Like knots in cotton.

Dot He can't help himself.

Vic *sings half a verse of 'You Make Me Feel So Young' to* **Dot**.

Liz Can he whistle? Because he can't sing.

John You tell him, Gran.

Vic I know, Ma, 'Over the Hills and Far Away'.

Liz Yes. That's where I want you to sing it. (*She begins to chuckle at her own joke and continues to laugh throughout the rest of the scene.*)

Doris Look at my mam. She's having a little titter to herself.

Dot Yeah, at Vic's expense.

Liz He thinks he's such a good singer.

Jack (*musing*) Do you know, that sun is lovely.

Dot Vic's as soft as a brush.

Liz He'll never be one of us though will he? He'll never be a member of this family, no matter how hard he tries.

Vic (*laughing, slightly hurt*)   This is my family, Ma. This is my family.

Liz   This is my family, Vic. This is my family and I love them all . . .

Dot (*warmly and kindly*)   Look at my mam, she's as pleased as punch.

Liz (*musing*)   Over the hills and far away . . . (*She begins to laugh.*)

The rest of the family join in the laughter; it should be the gentlest laugh possible. **Rebecca** *enters upstage with her clarinet; she plays Gershwin's 'Summertime' very movingly. The lights fade. There is the sound of birdsong.*

Curtain.

Act Two

Alma Cogan singing 'Why Do Fools Fall in Love?' plays. The cast enter and take up positions around the stage in a dim light. It is now nineteen seventy-five. **Dot** *is centre stage, sweeping dust into a dustpan. She is agitated.* **Vic** *is upstage, watching* **Dot**. **Liz** *sits in a chair upstage. Although the audience can see and hear her, she is, in fact, dead. The rest of the cast watch* **Dot**. **John** *wanders downstage, much more casually than before; he, too, watches* **Dot**. *The music fades. The lights come up on the scene. There is a silence.*

Dot I don't believe it!

Vic Look at you, you're killing yourself.

Dot After all we've done for him? I'm behind with my routine today.

Vic You don't have to do that every day.

Dot I've got all upstairs to do yet. There's no tea on; he's really upset me, he has.

Vic Why, what's he done?

Dot He knows I have a good tidy around on a Wednesday.

Vic You do the same every day.

Dot I'm finished at one on Tuesdays.

Vic (*in disbelief*) You do the *same* every day.

Dot He has to come and upset me on a Wednesday?

Vic It wouldn't matter which day he came; you do the same every day.

Dot (*ignoring* **Vic**) Sundays are usually my big day for washing.

Vic You wash every day. You can see through my

trousers because you wash them every day. You're washing away all our clothes.

Dot   There's no tea on.

Vic   I heard you the first time.

Dot (*flustered*)   So I don't know what you're going to have.

Vic   I'll have nothing.

Dot   You can't have nothing.

Vic   I'm not hungry.

Dot   You must be hungry.

Vic   How do you know if I'm hungry?

Dot   So you're not hungry?

Vic   I'm starving but I want to know what's been going on.

Dot *stops cleaning.*

Dot (*to* **John**)   Tell your dad.

John   You're the one making a song and a dance about it – you tell him.

Dot   Tell him!

John   No.

Dot   Tell him.

John   No.

Dot   He's been kicked out.

John   That's not true.

Dot   He's been kicked out because he's pathetic, and we'll be the laughing-stock . . . I can just see your Edna's face. I can just see her smug expression when she finds out. . . .

John   Mother, no one will be a laughing-stock, because it's not true. So, hard luck, you're wrong again, you're wrong, you're wrong, you're wrong.

Vic   Is it true?

John   No.

Dot (*in a rage*)   Tell him, tell your dad, because I'm disgusted with you, I am. I wash my hands of you. In fact I'll tell you something: I haven't got time for you. I'm finished with you. I don't care what you do. He knows what things are like with my nerves since my mam died. I'm finished with him, I am. Finished.

Liz *watches the action with interest.*

John   Great, well, thanks for your support. I'll not bother coming home again, it'll save all the hassle.

Dot   It'll suit me.

John   Will it?

Dot   It will.

John   You couldn't stop crying when I left.

Dot   I won't cry when you leave this time.

Liz *tuts audibly.*

John   Won't you?

Dot   No I won't. You can go now for me.

John   You'd have a stroke if I did.

Dot   I wouldn't.

John   You want to know my every move.

Dot   I don't.

John   Don't you? You could have fooled me.

Vic (*exhausted*)   Will somebody please talk to me?

John   It's my mother.

Liz   She's always been the same.

John   She's crackers.

Liz   She takes after her dad.

John (*moving to* **Vic***; controlled*)   It's no big deal, my
mother's getting carried away as usual, because she
only half listens to what anybody has to say. . . . Unless
you're talking about lace curtains or nylon sheets or
double glazing my mother's not interested. . . . She
ought to be on *Tomorrow's World* as an expert on dust.
(*To* **Dot**.) Why d'you clean up all the time?

Dot   Do you think I like it? Do you think I want to?
You'll come a cropper, you will.

John   Will I?

Dot   Yes.

John   I won't.

Dot   He's throwing opportunities away. I could have
gone to grammar school, you know, but we didn't
have any money to pay for me. What is there in my
bloody life? All I do is stay in this rotten house and
clean up. What have I got in my life?

Vic   I think I'll go out and come in again. It's like a
madhouse. I thought all the shouting and bawling was
a thing of the past. (*He walks about the stage, unable to bear
the emotional tension.*)

Dot   He's been thrown out of college. He's been
there a year, he's done no work. I could hit him.

John   That'd be helpful, wouldn't it?

Dot   Don't think I won't smack you, my lad.

John   Play something different, will you?

Dot (*becoming calmer*)   And shall I tell you why he's

been kicked out?

John Here we go, more lies.

Vic Let's listen.

Dot Because he can't keep away from the women.

There is a silence. **John** *looks slightly embarrassed.*

Dot Now?

There is another silence.

He can't control himself, that's the problem. He's always after the women.

Vic (*carefully*) Well don't look at me as if it's my fault.

Dot He can't control himself.

Vic That's not my fault.

Dot When he's away from home he thinks he's Errol Flynn.

John I don't.

Liz (*to herself*) I love Errol Flynn.

Dot He's done no work all year and we're living on tinned ham.

Liz (*to herself*) I love Errol Flynn . . .

Dot Living on tinned ham? If anybody knew.

Vic We're not *just* living on tinned ham.

Dot As soon as he gets with that lot he's in that college bar, drinking, messing about, making a fool of himself. I'll tell you this, we haven't sacrificed all we have for you to be sleeping with every girl you speak to.

John Where's all this come from?

Dot I knew as soon as I saw him.

John   What?

Dot   As soon as he came through that door I knew something had changed.

John   OK, so you're psychic.

Liz (*to* **John**)   He wants to watch what he's doing.

Dot   I'm your mother; I know you better than you know yourself.

John   You should have gone to college for me, then.

Vic   What he does in his own time is none of our business.

Dot   We don't know what he does.

John   Why has this come up?

Dot   You've been too soft with him, Vic.

Liz (*to* **Vic**)   He always has been.

Dot   He's failed everything.

John   I haven't.

Dot   We had that phone put in and he never rings. He should have gone down the pit like the rest of the family instead of thinking he was sommat special. All our family's worked at pit, on both sides. He's bloody disgrace, and he smells.

Vic (*to* **John**)   Have you?

John   What?

Liz   They should have hit him more often.

Dot   He has.

Vic (*shouting*)   Will you listen for a minute?

Liz (*to no one*)   Always shouting in that house.

Dot   It's him.

Liz He should have been a prison warden.

John OK, I failed my foundation course and Philosophy and that's about it.

Vic Right.

John And I failed the Sociology course.

Vic Right.

John And Education, Psychology and Maths.

Vic And what about Drama?

John I did all right, I got a C-minus.

Vic (*sarcastically*) Oh, congratulations, you must be over the moon.

John All I have to do, and I've been trying to explain this to my mother, is submit a piece of work and they'll accept me back. I've written a play and it can be used as part of the course work. I've been upset about my gran an' all, you know, I couldn't work; all I could do was my play.

Vic Right, now we know. (*He calms down.*) We've all been upset. Now, what's it about, this here play?

There is a pause.

John It's about a night club.

Vic About bloody . . . who's gunna be interested in that? And that's going to get you back to be a teacher, is it? You're bloody barmy, you're living in cloud-cuckoo-land. You listen to me: stop living life in the fast lane.

John Teacher training college is hardly the fast lane.

Vic I don't want any lip.

John I didn't go to drama school because of you.

Vic It's sommat to fall back on, we all agreed on

that, now you know we did.

Dot   He's disco mad.

John   I like to watch.

Dot   He's one of them perverts.

Vic   Can we just . . . hang on . . . can we leave it?
Now I've had a day of it at work and all. So why
don't we all help your mother get finished cleaning up,
and then we'll have some tea.

Dot   It's only tinned ham.

Vic (*sarcastically*)   I love tinned ham.

John (*to the audience*)   My dad could eat anything, he
had bionic teeth. He needn't have bothered taking the
ham out of the tin, he could bite straight through it.

Vic (*histrionically*)   I loved tinned ham.

Vic *exits.* **Dot** *exits. The lights change.* **John** *turns to address
the audience.*

John (*to the audience*)   It was nineteen seventy-five and
a lot of things had changed. For a start I'd got a brace
of A levels and a place at teacher's training college.
And my mother was right, I'd lost my virginity. In fact
I lost my virginity as many times as I could. (*He pauses.*)
College was great because nobody died and the future
as a teacher of Drama looked bright and secure. And
as my Aunt Edna had said, 'It was something to fall
back on.' Back at home my grandad had moved in
with us. Gran had died.

Liz *gets up. Only* **John** *can see her.*

Liz (*after a pause, to* **John**)   I went in for a
hysterectomy, but it was too much. It was a nice quiet
funeral. But the weather was awful. A small family
affair, with a small reception at our Dorothy's. I was
surprised Ken actually made it. But I suppose he had

to; our Doris was in such a state she couldn't walk. I warned 'em. When you love like we did ... (*She returns to her seat to watch the action.*)

Vic, **Jack** *and* **Dot** *enter.* **Jack** *is carrying a pair of garden shears.* **Doris** *enters to them.*

Doris   I've put some flowers on my mam's, Dot. I've been down to the ... you know? I've put some new flowers on. We can take turns, putting them on.

Dot   Are you all right, Dad? Are you going to sit down for a minute and have a sandwich?

Jack   I'm all right. These shears need seeing to.

Dot   You look a bit flushed.

Jack   I'm right.

Doris   Come and sit down, Dad.

Jack   I don't like to sit. My mind thinks on it when I sit; I like to keep moving.

Doris   He doesn't like going to the ... you know?

Vic   You'll tire yourself out.

Jack (*close to tears*)   It's just that ...

Dot   We know, Dad, we know ...

Doris   Don't ...

Jack   When I see the garden, when I see the sun on the garden, I think ... I can't help it.

Vic   Hey, come on.

Jack *completely breaks down, crying the cry of a man who has never cried and does not want to. The rest of the family is on the verge of breaking down too.*

Jack   I'm sorry ... I'm sorry ... Oh God, Dot, I wish she was back ... I do.

Dot   I know.

Jack   I wish she was back . . .

Doris   Don't, Dad.

Jack   Oh . . . why didn't He take me?

Dot   Come on . . .

Liz   Then I'd've been left on my own.

The family sits **Jack** *down and comforts him.*

Jack   She must have been in such pain. For years –
and she never told anyone.

Dot   I know, I know.

Jack   Why didn't He take me?

Liz   He was always selfish.

Jack   Oh, I miss her.

Doris   He's setting me off.

Jack   I can't help it.

Dot   I miss her too.

Jack   I miss her.

They all start to cry, or are near to tears.

Liz   My family.

John   Don't cry, Grandad.

Dot   Oh, Mother. (*She hugs* **John**, *crying.*) Oh Mam,
my mam, I miss her, John, I miss her.

John (*comforting* **Dot**)   I know, Mam, I know.

Jack (*attempting to compose himself*)   Do you know what's
the worse thing? I never told her I loved her. She
never knew.

Vic   I miss her.

There is a silence.

Liz I never thought I'd hear Vic say that.

Dot She knew.

Jack No.

Dot She did.

Jack I never told her.

Vic She knew, Pa, you didn't have to tell her.

Jack I did. But I was too bloody bull-headed.

Doris She knew.

Liz I knew, Jack.

Jack If she was here now I'd tell her. . . .

Dot No, you wouldn't, you'd be out in the garden pottering about or watching the racing, and that's what she'd expect you to do. My mam was like me; she didn't go in for all that lovey-dovey stuff.

Liz It would have been nice once in a while.

Doris Eh, come on Dad, she wouldn't want you to be ruining your life, would she?

Dot No, she wouldn't, she wouldn't've wanted that. . . .

Doris No, she wouldn't.

Dot Get some fresh air. I'll get his coat.

Dot *exits.*

Doris Why don't you take him a walk, Vic?

Jack, *recovering, wipes his tears away with a white handkerchief, watched by the others.*

Vic Do you want to go a walk, Pa?

They all freeze, holding the moment. The lights change. **John** *breaks out of the freeze.*

John (*to the audience*)   And they walked around the block, and played cards, and talked, and drank tea, and cut the lawn, and listened to records and drank more tea, and dunked ginger biscuits. But the pain was too deep. It was rooted, you could almost see it. You could touch it with your fingers. It had a hold of my grandad and was pulling him down, forcing him nearer to the ground, twisting him like the stump of an old tree. And they walked and drank tea and listened to records, and I wondered how many hands of pontoon you have to play to erase sixty years of love. I thought the pain would be over in a blink, but I was wrong – it was with us for ever.

John *returns to his place in the frozen scene. The lights change. It is now a few months later.* **Dot** *enters, full of energy. She addresses the whole family.*

Dot   Do you know what I've been thinking?

Vic   What do you think we are, mind-readers?

Dot   Don't you think it would be nice if we all went away together this summer?

John (*frightened*)   Eh?

Dot   All of us.

John   The whole family?

Dot   I think we should go away.

Vic   We could visit our Edna in Gloucester.

John   And slash our wrists.

Doris   Go away where?

Dot   Well, we can't take my dad to Blackpool, so I thought we'd have a change.

Liz   He loves Blackpool; take him to Blackpool.

Doris   A change?

Dot   I thought it would be really good if we all went in a caravan.

John (*horrified*)   Eh?

Dot   All the family together like old times. We could get a six-berth at Feathers in Whitley Bay.

John   Me as well?

Dot   All of us.

Liz   Good idea. You need a break. Get you out of that house.

Jack   Well, I don't know.

Doris (*loudly, as if* **Jack** *is deaf*)   It'll be a change, Dad. A change.

John   I'm not going.

Dot   Why not?

John   I don't want to.

Dot   Can't you just do it for us?

John   Oh yes, it sounds wonderful, doesn't it?

Doris   It'll be cosy.

John   Like living in a lift.

Liz (*to herself*)   I've always liked Geordies.

John   Yes, but can you imagine it?

Vic   I think your grandad would like it, kid.

John   Tough.

Jack (*slowly*)   He doesn't have to come for me.

John   See.

Dot   He's coming.

John　I'm not.

Liz　Lovely people they are, Geordies.

Doris　I think it'll be good.

John　A week in a caravan?

Doris　Yes. Sounds exciting; I like caravanning.

John　I'd rather be buried alive.

Vic　It could be arranged.

John　My dad's a funny man, give him a round of applause.

Dot　Stop it, you. Who do you think you are?

John　I'm me, who're you?

Vic　Oh, we're off?

John　Yeah, we are.

Doris　What's wrong with him?

Liz　He's on drugs.

Dot　He's crackers.

John　Listen who's talking. I don't wash the curtains fifteen times a day. Why don't we become nudists? It would help my mother's arthritis.

Jack (*cautiously, as if sensing a row brewing*)　I think I'll have a walk.

Dot　It's raining, Dad.

Jack　I think I'll have a little stroll.

John　What, another?

Vic　Just stop it.

Liz　He wants belting when he's like that.

Jack　He should have had more belts, he should.

John   That's your answer to everything, isn't it? If it moves, hit it.

Doris   Come on, kid. Uncle Ken might come.

Jack   If he's going, I'm not.

Doris   Come on, the whole family. Your gran'd like it.

John   My gran's dead.

Liz *tuts audibly.*

Dot   He's selfish.

John   Me?

Dot   You.

Vic   I think we've heard enough.

John   *Selfish.* Hang on! You look no interest in my school work. All you said was 'Get it done.' You didn't even let me do my homework at the dinner table, you said it was too messy. I revised for my A levels in the loo.

Vic   Why do you exaggerate every-bloody-thing?

Dot   He's changed.

John   How very observant.

Vic   Let it drop.

Liz   I think it would be nice, a few days by the sea.

Dot   He's changed, and it's not for the better.

Jack *(as if lost)*   I'll get some fresh air.

Doris   It's throwing it down.

Jack   I'll cut your hedges.

Vic   It's raining, Pa.

Jack   It'll not take long.

Vic Pa?

John There's no hedges left, he cuts them every day.

Jack I'll just trim 'em.

John The grass is taller than the privets.

Dot I never thought I'd see a son of mine wearing mascara.

John I wondered how long it would be before that came up.

Dot Mascara!

John I only wore it for a laugh.

Doris What's he been wearing mascara for?

John A laugh.

Vic He's crackers.

Jack I don't want to be in a caravan with him if he's wearing make-up.

John I'm not; my mother's got the wrong end of the stick . . . again.

Liz He should never have gone away.

Dot And I'll tell you something else while I'm at it. Don't think we don't know when you're lying to us.

John OK, I admit it. I'm a member of the KGB.

Dot He lies, he does, Doris.

Doris (*philosophically*) Everybody does.

Dot 'Don't come and see me at college, Mother, I'm busy'; 'Don't come that week I'm doing something'; 'No, I can't come home, I'm rehearsing' . . . I was surprised you made it to the funeral.

Liz She goes too far.

John   Look, you reap what you sow. You pushed me, you wanted me to go away, and, all right, maybe I've changed, but so what? And what makes you think that being a close family and not changing is so wonderful? Look at yourselves: what makes you think you're all so perfect that there's no room for change?

Vic   Well, if wearing make-up is a change for the better you can stick it.

John   Look at this house.

Liz   It's a lovely house.

John   You're never out of it. You wear it like a coffin. It's suffocating you.

Dot   That's why we want to go away.

John   Into a caravan or a boarding house? It's the same thing . . . it's *worse!*

Liz   I always wanted to stay at the Metropole.

John (*to* **Jack**)   And look at him.

Liz   But we never did.

John   Jack the lad. How long is he going to sit and mope about my gran? (*To* **Jack**.) Hey, you, let's have a box, now, shall we, just me and you; you'd be wheezing like an old fart.

Vic   John?

John (*to* **Jack**)   Did you think she'd never die? Because you're acting like you never expected it to happen. She's been dead nearly a year.

Liz (*to* **John**)   Nine months . . . I've been dead nine months, don't exaggerate.

Doris   Nine months.

Liz   Thank you.

Dot (*to* **John**)   Can you hear what you're saying?

John   For nine months he's been walking about as though dead lice were dropping off him. I thought he was supposed to be a hard nut.

Vic   Don't be bloody pathetic.

John   Hey, Dad, don't get carried away; your false teeth might drop out.

Vic   Stop it.

John   Might give us all a nasty bite.

Doris   All this over a holiday?

Vic   I won't forget you for that.

Dot   It's been coming this has, Doris, it's been coming for ages.

John   My dad's got the most frightening false teeth in Europe.

Vic   I won't forget you for that.

John   I've heard you.

Dot   He knows this family's still upset but he's not bothered about anybody but himself. He knows what the situation's like with my dad living here and he's not bothered.

John   Why is he here? Why doesn't he go back to his own house?

Doris   He doesn't like it there on his own.

Liz (*easily*)   Too many memories.

Dot   He's not bothered.

John   No, I'm not. You're right, for once. In fact, do you want to know something?

Vic   Here we go.

John   I wish you were *all* dead. All of you –

Dot   We will be if you keep on. He's driving me to my grave.

John   – because we'll never be free until we're born from test tubes. And maybe one day you'll understand what I'm on about.

Doris   You've got your whole life ahead of you; one week in a caravan isn't going to hurt.

Vic   I don't understand him.

John   I don't want to spend one day in a caravan. Not with you, nor my dad, or the Queen, the Pope or anybody. I couldn't think of anything more horrible than a week in Whitley Bay. And while I'm on my hobby-horse let me tell you for the millionth time that I don't like cheese and egg when it's cooked in the oven, or fry-up, or bacon and tomato dip or tinned bloody ham. All right, Mother? Do you understand? The world is a big place, it's even bigger than this house.

Liz   I always fancied Greece.

John   And if you lot want to go and sit in a box on Tyneside watching the rain, and playing happy families, and listening to my mother go on and on about the price increases in Marks and Spencer's and how she can't get her curtains to hang straight, then go, go now. And if you fancy walking with him (*He indicates* **Jack**.) to St Mary's lighthouse and back a million times a day talking about what my gran would have thought about it, good for you. But I'm not. I refuse my consent and, no matter what you say, nothing, and I mean nothing, will change my mind.

Dot   Don't come then.

Liz   He's changed, he has. I liked him better when he was younger . . . He was always a nice little lad; he was the apple of his gran's eye.

Doris   Well.

Doris *stands, saying nothing, then exits.*

Vic   Now we know.

Jack   I think I'll get a blow of fresh air.

Dot   It's still raining, Dad.

Jack   Shall I make us all a cuppa tea?

Vic (*shouting*)   Just sit down, Jack. (*Calmly.*) Let's sort this one out.

Dot (*to* **John**, *pleadingly*)   Will you come?

John   No.

Dot   Please, kid, please.

John   No. I'll never go on holiday with you again, ever.

The lights change; we are on the beach at Whitley Bay. It is evening. The sounds of a high wind and stormy sea can be heard. All exit except **Jack**, **Liz** *and* **John**. **Liz** *hands* **Jack** *a coat, which he puts on.* **John** *puts on a windjammer.* **Jack** *is stoic and silent.*

John   Not a bad caravan, is it? Cramped but cosy.

Jack *is silent; his face shows his reactions to* **John**'s *speech, though his mind is with* **Liz**.

John   Came down here yesterday. Nice, i'n't it? After we played snap and that. I came down for a read. Heavy stuff; Camus, *A Happy Death.*

Jack *is still silent.*

John   Not many laughs. (*To the audience.*) No man ever used silences like my grandad, he made Pinter seem loquacious.

There is a silence.

John (*to* **Jack**)   All that sea?

Jack *does not respond.*

John   A boat there, look.

Again, **Jack** *does not respond.*

John   I use them weights, you know? I've got them in my room at college.

There is a silence.

Jack   I was never right by her. I never did anything right. (*Pause.*) I was never any good around the house. (*Pause.*) She bought a wardrobe. And we couldn't get it upstairs. So I sawed the banister rail off. She went mad.

Liz (*enjoying the memory*)   I can remember.

Jack (*after a pause*)   Look after your mother if anything happens. (*He pauses.*) There's a blank space on the headstone. It's like an open bible. Liz's name is on one side, the other's a blank, just waiting for me.

There is a silence. **Jack** *and* **John** *hardly look at one another.*

Jack   Don't ever forget where you came from.

John   No.

There is another silence.

Jack   I never knew my mother.

John   No.

Jack   I didn't belong anywhere.

John   No.

Jack   She calmed me down.

John   Yes.

Jack   I had a job as a grocer's lad when I first saw her. (*His voice softens.*) Never forget where you come from.

John   I don't feel like I belong at college. Everybody seems really clever. Makes me feel stupid.

Jack   Ar?

John   And I don't belong at home any more.

Jack (*as if his mind is drifting*)   No.

John   We had this discussion the other week about whether a rational man should ever hit anybody. This tutor got me so wound up, I could have hit him.

Jack   Tha should have.

John (*after a pause*)   I'm sorry about what I said back home. It was pathetic.

Jack   Ar.

John   Is it true, didn't you have a family?

Jack   I had a stepfather. One day he took a belt to me in the street. I never forgot that. When I was twenty-one, I took him into the street and gave him a hiding. Don't ever trust anybody. And if people think bad of you give them good reason to think it. You've done well. I never expected thee to go as far as you have, it's sommat I don't understand. Thee just remember two generations ago this family had nothing.

John   Sounds like a Dickens novel.

Jack   I'm serious.

There is another long silence.

He's still around, that Davis.

John   I'm not interested.

Jack   Married now.

John   Good for him.

Jack   Eric Allport's daughter. He was up in court last month.

John (*as if uninterested*)   Oh . . . ?

Jack   It was in the paper. Gone into somebody's house where his ex-wife was staying with her new fancy man and broke his nose.

John   I think the wind's getting up.

Jack   Hit 'em while they're taking their coats off. One-two. . . . The whole family are scum.

John   Well, we can't all be brain surgeons.

Jack   Scum.

John   They're probably all right you know, really.

Jack   They're a bad lot. He had a baby to Lyn Sutton. Then he left her.

John   Well, that's all behind me now.

Jack   A quick one-two. And it's over.

John   Live and let live.

Liz   You'd better go back, Jack.

There is a silence.

Don't want you catching a chill.

There is a silence.

Best get back and then our Dot'll make you some supper.

Jack   I miss her.

The lights change, bathing the stage in blue. The sound of the wind gets louder. **John**, **Liz** *and* **Jack** *are 'blown' off the stage.* **Dot**, **Edna**, **Vic** *and* **Rebecca** *are 'blown' on to the stage. The wind noise fades. The lights come up on the house* *once more. The family is having tea.* **Dot** *stands near the doorway, as if she is about to exit into the kitchen. She appears to be agitated.*

Dot   Does anybody want Branston Pickle?

Vic   We love it up there, Edna.

Rebecca   In a caravan?

Vic   We love caravanning.

Dot   Does anyone want any corned beef?

Rebecca   Isn't it overpowering, Uncle Vic?

Edna   I don't think I'd like a caravan holiday.

Vic   That's what our John thought.

Edna   No. It would be too claustrophobic for me.

Rebecca   Mother doesn't like to be hemmed in.

Dot   Spring onions, anybody?

Vic   We love it.

Dot   Does anyone want any luncheon meat? I've got some.

Vic (*to* **Dot**)   I'll have a piece of that blackberry pie afterwards.

Dot   You won't. The pieces stick in his teeth, Edna.

John (*to the audience*)   I'd just finished my final year's teaching practice when Burke and Hare dropped in on us for a surprise visit.

Dot   Are you sure you've had enough, Edna?

Edna   Absolutely.

Dot   Would you like another piece of ham? It's lean. I got it from Denis Richards. His mother's blind. The butcher. Nice man, isn't he, Vic?

Edna No, thank you, Dorothy.

Dot Are you sure? You've hardly eaten anything. Nice man. Eh, Vic?

Vic His mother's blind, Edna. She's eighty-five.

Dot Rebecca, go on, have a bite.

John (*to the family*) She still hasn't got over that tart.

Vic And that was five years ago.

Dot Go on, it'll not kill you.

Rebecca No, I'm fine.

Edna Rebecca doesn't eat meat.

Dot Oh, is she ill?

Rebecca No, I –

Dot (*to* **John**) We like to eat, don't we, kid?

John Yeah, even when we're not hungry.

Dot I'll save this up for tomorrow then, our John can have it in a fry-up.

John (*to the audience*) Fry-up?

Dot I love it when he's at home, Edna, college holidays, I love it.

Dot *exits*.

Vic So what's new in the world, Rebecca? Not shooting off to India again, are we?

Rebecca Not any more, Uncle Vic. I'm working as a nursery nurse and Mike and I are very happy.

John What does Mike do?

Rebecca He's a doctor. Mercury research. I'm not sure of the detail. Atmosphere pollution, that sort of thing.

Edna   Rebecca is her own person, Vic; she had a career ahead of her and she's just let it go.

Vic   Well, if it's what she wants.

Rebecca   I had to let it go. I wasn't good enough, so I stopped. I've explained this to my mother a thousand times.

Vic   Are we likely to see a wedding in the family soon?

Rebecca   That's a touchy subject, Uncle Vic.

Edna   I don't like them living together.

Vic   Well, that's what they do nowadays. I wish me and Dot had had a trial period. It would have saved all this heartache over the last twenty years.

Rebecca   You don't mean that.

John   He does.

Vic   I do. (*He crouches on the floor to eat.*)

Dot *enters*.

Dot   Don't sit like that, Vic, you'll get indigestion. Sit up properly when you eat.

Rebecca   My mother's one of the two remaining eminent Victorians.

John   My mother's the other.

Edna (*ignoring the bait*)   I would have some more tea, Dorothy. It's lovely tea.

Dot   It's Early Grey, our John likes it.

John   I'm trying to educate them.

Vic (*sarcastically*)   He thinks we need it.

Edna   It really is lovely tea, I don't think I've ever had it before.

Rebecca   You have, Mum.

Edna   Have I?

Rebecca   Mike and I have it.

John   I went to Benidorm on an 'Eighteen-to-Thirty' holiday last summer.

Rebecca   Oh, how awful.

Edna   Did you have to go? Was it part of the course or something?

John   No. I went because it was cheap.

Vic   He flew out and then went around Europe.

Dot   He's completely insane, our John, Edna, don't you know?

John   It was great.

Dot   I don't mind Early Grey.

Rebecca   Oh, I couldn't.

John   No, you might meet a working-class person and we couldn't have that.

Rebecca   What do you think I was doing in India? The people there had nothing.

John   There are people here with nothing.

Vic (*easily*)   Yes, us, we've got nothing, Rebecca. We're living on tinned ham at the moment.

Dot   Sit up, Vic.

Edna   No, I don't like Spain: too sticky.

Dot   We've never been.

Vic   We've been to Eastbourne.

Dot   I like Eastbourne.

John   I went up to Madrid, have you been?

Rebecca No.

John Saw *Guernica* at the Prado, have you seen it?

Rebecca No.

Dot I like Eastbourne ... and Whitley Bay.

John It's massive.

Dot Eastbourne's not too big. But it's a long drive.

John Then I went to Toledo and I hitched across Europe.

Edna I don't like Spain.

John Did you see the Dali exhibition?

Rebecca No.

Vic *sips his tea and makes a noise.*

Dot Don't make a noise when you drink your tea, Vic, it's rude.

Vic I'm not.

Dot You are.

John Is there any biscuits?

Dot Have you ever been to Eastbourne?

Edna No.

Dot We like it, don't we, Vic?

Vic Eastbourne?

Dot We like it.

Edna Never been.

Dot Sit up, Vic.

John I didn't know that Kokoschka and Hitler applied for the same course at art school, did you, Rebecca?

Rebecca (*surprised*)   No.

Dot   He makes a noise with his false teeth, don't you, Vic? I think his gums must have shrunk, and when he drinks he makes a noise. It sounds like his teeth are rattling around in his head.

Edna   I see.

Dot   Awful in public.

Vic   Our John's trying to make us more cultured, Rebecca.

Rebecca   Good. Educating you, is he? You should travel, Uncle Vic.

Dot   I don't like what he likes, I think it's rubbish.

Vic   It's different.

Dot   I'm getting awful pains in my chest, Edna.

Vic   He treated us to the theatre for my birthday.

Dot   It was awful.

Vic   It was at the Grand. Terry Griffiths. *The Comedians*. I thought it was fantastic.

Rebecca   Did you see the Jasper Johns exhibition?

John   Yeah, I thought it was crap.

Rebecca   Really?

John   I didn't see it.

Dot   I like Donald O'Connor.

John   My mother likes the musicals.

Dot   I don't like what he likes.

John   Trevor, Dad.

Vic   Trevor Griffiths, that's it.

John   So you're co-habiting, Rebecca?

Rebecca At the moment.

Edna (*changing the subject*) You've got a wonderful garden still, Dorothy.

Dot My dad sees to it.

Edna How is he?

Dot He's moved in permanently now. The house was too much for him.

Rebecca Have you sold the house?

Vic It was council, Rebecca.

Rebecca Really?

Vic Yeah, it was a council house.

John That means you have to pay rent.

Dot We don't see much of him. He comes in for his dinner, then goes for a walk, then he comes back for his tea. Then he goes and sits at the bottom of the street. He counts the cars. Then he comes in and reads a cowboy book.

Vic He doesn't like to be a nuisance.

Dot He isn't.

Vic No I'm not saying he is.

Rebecca So what's next for John?

John I'm going to the moon.

Rebecca You've really changed in the last few years.

John Do you think so?

Rebecca Don't you think so, Mum?

Edna Well, he's certainly got bigger.

Vic He's written some plays, Rebecca, did you know?

Edna I hope they have a story.

Rebecca   Mum hates *Godot*.

Vic   He's sent one to Yorkshire telly.

John   I haven't heard owt.

Edna   I used to like the theatre, but I don't go now. Plays today are so depressing.

Rebecca   It's quite amazing – the difference.

Dot   We don't know who he is half the time. He's crackers.

Vic   He's doing an extra year.

Dot   I don't know where he gets his brains from.

Vic   He gets them from my side of the family, Rebecca.

Rebecca (*to* **John**)   Yes you've changed.

Doris *and* **Jack** *enter. They have obviously been walking vigorously.* **Jack** *looks flushed but not ill;* **Doris** *is lively and cheerful.*

Jack   Ar . . . that's better. Bit of fresh air.

Doris   Just been for a walk.

John (*to* **Rebecca**)   Did you think I'd always be eleven?

Rebecca   Not exactly.

Doris   It's ever so close outside.

Jack   A walk, lovely. Take the dogs, stretch their legs.

Doris   It's muggy, close. We've had a nice stroll, haven't we? Down to the . . . you know.

Dot   How are the flowers?

Doris   They look lovely, don't they? Looks really nice.

Jack *and* **Doris** *sit down;* **Liz** *watches them.*

John (*to* **Rebecca**) Whenever you come here you make me mam 'n' dad feel inferior, did you know that?

Vic John?

John It's true.

Vic Take no notice of him, Rebecca.

Rebecca Well, if I did, I never intended to.

John Well, that's how it is. The best china always comes out when you're here.

Doris It's special, isn't it?

Edna (*changing the subject*) How's Grandad?

Jack Tired.

Edna I was just saying that the garden is as lovely as ever.

Jack What?

Vic The garden –

Edna It's as lovely as ever.

Jack Nice little piece of God's earth.

Dot I was on about Eastbourne.

Doris I don't like it.

Vic I knew she'd say that.

Dot She doesn't like it.

Edna I was saying: I've never been.

Doris No.

Edna No.

Doris No . . . I don't like it. Too quiet.

Dot   She likes a bit of life.

Doris   I like a bit of life.

Doris *exits to the garden.*

John   It must be me; I over-compensate.

Rebecca   What for?

John   My dismal failures.

Rebecca   I've never thought of you like that.

Vic   He's a slow starter.

John   Look out for the joke.

Vic   It's not a joke, he's a slow starter. Like I am.

John   He means late developer.

Rebecca   You were just different to us, that's all. I never saw it in any other way.

John   We had nothing in common.

Doris *enters.*

Doris   It's muggy, you know what I mean? Muggy. Your clothes stick to you. Muggy.

Dot   I don't like it when it's muggy.

John   Now I've got nothing in common with my mam and dad.

Vic   He has.

John   I haven't.

Jack   Is there any corned beef?

Dot   Do you want some?

Jack   I'll have some. After.

Vic   Dot's dad's always doing that. He asks for something, she gets up, then he says, 'I'll have some after.'

Dot Do you want any corned beef, nip?

Doris I don't like it. Gives me heartburn. I want a rest. My dad's walked me to death.

Edna Has he?

Jack I haven't.

Doris He has . . .

Dot Don't let him overdo it.

Edna Be careful you know, be careful.

Vic He's as fit as a fiddle, aren't you, Pa?

Jack (*easily*) I'm not.

Vic He's as fit as a fiddle.

Dot You shouldn't let him overdo it, Doris.

Jack I'm as fit as a fiddle.

John We eat off the floor when you're not here, we don't even have plates.

Dot He's crackers.

Vic It's clean enough.

Dot Oh, he's off again.

John My mother's doing a university degree, Rebecca, did you know? In cleaning up.

Vic She's a BC: Bachelor of Cleaning.

Dot I need a VC living with you lot.

John I'm off for a shit.

John *exits. Dogs can be heard barking in the distance.*

Doris Very close. And the litter, have you seen it? (*To* **Dot**.) Hear, can you hear?

Dot   What is it?

Doris   The dogs are barking; they need a drink.

Vic   I can't hear anything.

Dot   Our Doris can hear 'em. She knows them dogs.

Doris   They're barking, they want something.

Jack (*getting up*)   Have they had a drink? I'll do it.

Dot   Have a minute, Dad, they're our Doris's dogs.

Vic   Sit down, Pa.

Doris   They need a drink.

Doris *exits*.

Jack   I'll do it. She can't be doing it all.

Vic   Sit.

Dot   They're her dogs.

Vic   Rover, stay.

Dot   They're a nuisance, them dogs.

Vic   Dot? Don't.

Dot (*becoming anxious*)   Our Doris thinks more about them dogs than she does about people. She talks to them.

Vic   Oh, she's off: 'My nerves are bad.'

Dot   She makes me sick, she does. Always on about them dogs.

Vic   Her nerves are bad, Edna.

Edna   How are your hands, Dorothy?

Vic   They're bad, Edna, she can't keep her hands out of water.

Dot (*showing* **Edna** *her hands*)   Look. Arthritis. And my nerves.

Vic   She'll get that all through her body.

Dot   My mother had it, all through her body.

Edna   Your mother had cancer as well, though, didn't she?

Dot   I sometimes wonder.

Vic   She worries herself.

Dot   I think about it . . . awful pains in my back. Awful. And my nerves . . . shocking, Edna.

Vic   She worries herself sick about it. I've told her to see a specialist.

Edna   I know . . . You should see someone.

Vic   We're dropping to bits, Rebecca.

Rebecca   Young at heart, though, Uncle Vic.

Vic   That's us, young at heart. But you've got to be, Rebecca. Look at me, I'm crawling about all day on my hands and knees following a machine; you've got to be young inside.

Rebecca   At least you'll always have a job, Uncle Vic. Count your blessings. We're not sure how long Mike's research post will last.

Vic   That's the only good thing about it. There'll allus be coal around here.

Doris *enters.*

Doris   They've had a drink, that's what they wanted, they wanted a drink. I heard all that barking and I thought, 'I wonder what they want?' I thought my dad had given them a drink, and he thought I had, and neither of us had. Anyway . . .

Vic   They've had one now.

Dot They've got a dog next door, Edna. All day long, yap yap yap.

Edna I don't think I could stand it.

Vic A collie, a border collie.

Edna I like the quiet.

Doris You get used to it.

Dot Yap yap, gets on my nerves.

Vic Dot's nerves are bad.

Dot Yap yap . . . I don't know why our Doris brings 'em up.

Doris My dad likes to walk 'em. That's why I bring 'em.

Dot She brings 'em with her, they mess on the lawn.

Doris I only bring 'em for my dad, our Dorothy.

Dot I don't mind barking, but I can't stand the yapping.

Doris You've no need to worry, I won't bring them again.

Dot It'll suit me.

Doris I'll not bother coming if you want.

Vic Take no notice, Doris, she's all wound up.

Dot She won't, Edna. You can't talk to our Doris.

Dot *exits.*

Doris And what if I end up like my mother?

Doris *exits.*

Edna Better to be on the safe side.

Vic (*shouting*) Dogs do bark!

Rebecca (*to* **Edna**)   You have had Earl Grey.

Edna   I don't remember.

Rebecca   You had it when you visited Mike and I in Newbury.

Rebecca *exits.*

Edna   I did not!

Edna *exits.*

Vic (*shouting*)   Dogs do bark!

Jack   Vic's right.

Jack *exits.*

Vic   That's the first time you've agreed with me, Jack, in twenty-five years.

Vic *exits. There is a silence.* **John** *and* **Liz** *enter.* **John** *is wearing his graduation suit, as at the beginning of the play.* **Liz** *begins dusting the furniture used when the family were having tea, and returning the items to their original positions, if necessary.*

Liz   I never liked it when they came to visit. I always liked to keep out of the way. And that tea service, did you see that? I bought that. It was a wedding present. (*She pauses.*) I bet you didn't know that I'd paid for my own funeral.

John   I never really thought.

Liz   Of course you didn't, you were too busy floating about in a world of your own. You never really bothered about us, not since you went to comprehensive school.

John   That's not true.

Liz   Self, self, self.

John   I wanted to do well.

Liz   I'd have been proud of you if you'd been a vagrant.

John   Well, why didn't somebody say something?

Liz   It's your dad, always pushing.

John   It wasn't his fault.

There is a silence.

Liz   Did your mother get my records?

John   She plays them all the time.

Liz   I had nearly five hundred of them in my loft.
I'd saved them up over the years, seventy-eights they
were. I used to play them to you. Draw the curtains
on a Sunday afternoon, and have an ice cream.

John   'But don't tell your mother.'

Liz   That was it. And we'd listen to the records. Kay
Starr, Alma Cogan.

John (*remembering*)   Kay Starr, 'Bonaparte's Retreat'.

Liz   Uncle Ken bought me that, it was his favourite
... (*She pauses thoughtfully.*) Your mother said I spoilt
you.

John   You did.

Liz   Well, that's what grandparents are supposed to
do.

John (*surprised*)   Is it?

Liz   He always wanted a son.

John   Is that why?

Liz (*as if her mind is drifting*)   Always wanted a son.

John   We've always been nearer to your side of the
family, haven't we?

Liz   Vic's mother died when he was very young.

John   I didn't know that.

Liz His dad married again; she had children of her own. I don't think they were fair on Vic.

John You never liked my dad, did you?

Liz Vic was all right. Too wishy-washy for me. He wants everybody to like him. And they would if he didn't try so hard.

There is a silence.

John I couldn't get back, you know, at the end. I was at college. I couldn't get away.

Liz You could have.

John I had my finals.

Liz He was all right.

John Was he?

Liz Tough to the last.

John Yeah.

Liz He never made a fuss. Never once made a fuss. Did you?

Jack *enters. He has his hair slicked back and almost looks younger than he did when we last saw him. He, too, is dead, but moves about the stage quite normally. He kisses* **Liz** *on the cheek.*

Jack No.

Liz (*as if her mind is drifting*) Never once made a fuss.

Jack No.

Liz He did everything he wanted to. (*To* **Jack**.) Didn't you?

Jack Ar.

Liz He did what he wanted.

Jack Ar.

Liz   And he didn't let anybody pick on him.

Jack   No.

Liz   No regrets.

Jack   I left eight hundred pounds.

Liz   Well, you couldn't bring it with you.

Jack   Eight hundred.

Liz   Was everything else paid for? All the arrangements?

Jack   Ar.

Liz   Good. I didn't want our two to have unnecessary trouble.

Jack   I saved it up for a rainy day.

Liz   It'll come in handy. They could split it. Our Dot could get some new curtains.

Jack   They looked after me. Our Dot bathed me, dressed me, fed me and tucked me up in bed. They looked after me, they did.

Liz   They're two grand lasses.

Jack   They are.

There is a silence.

Liz   You know what I regret, Jack?

Jack   What's that, Liz?

Liz   I never went abroad, not in all my life. I never went abroad.

John (*to the audience*)   My mother and Aunty Doris were gutted when my grandad died, and it was the first time I'd seen my dad cry. Jack had a violent stroke – it didn't surprise me, everything he did was violent – and after months of my mam and Doris nursing him, and me trying to massage life into his now sparrow-like legs, he passed away. Fifty-two years of pit work had finally killed him. I stayed on an extra year and magically turned a lowly teaching certificate into a degree. It was nineteen seventy-eight, and I remember seeing Geek Davis. He was married now; they had two kids and he was as round as a beach ball. As we passed in the street Geek nodded and said, 'Hello'. I said nothing. I turned, grabbed him by the throat and hit him full in the face; he fell to the floor like a sack of shit . . . and as he looked up at me, his wife screaming and babies shouting, I kicked him full in the chest.

Jack   Yes, give him what for!

Liz   What are you playing at, you're supposed to be educated!

John (*to the audience*)   I know. For two months after I felt so pathetic that I didn't go out of the house.

The lights change. It is now nineteen seventy-eight. **Vic** *enters, wearing a smart suit. He is close to tears.*

Vic   Oh . . . fantastic, wasn't it? Ha, ha, I knew you'd do it. Jarring Jack Jackson.

Liz   He's on about that film again.

Jack   What film?

Liz   *That's My Boy*: Jerry Lewis.

Jack   I never liked him, he's like a nancy.

Liz   He was always going on about that film.

Vic (*to* **John**)   When I saw you up there with them others, oh, I was proud.

John   You were the only one who clapped.

Vic   I was proudish.

John That's not a word, Dad.

Vic It is.

John No, it's not.

Vic It is, proudish.

John (*anxiously*) It isn't a proper word, Dad.

Vic It is ... it is ...

John All right, it is then.

Vic Proudish is a word. Somewhat proud. I looked it up. Proudish.

John Where, *Reader's Digest*?

Vic Dictionary.

John Why did you stand up and clap?

Vic I just did.

John I know, I saw you. Two thousand people and you arc the only one to give a standing ovation. It's embarrassing.

Vic Don't start today.

John It was bloody embarrassing. And my mother. What was she playing at? I wish you'd never come.

Vic It was our day.

John I wish I'd never gone.

Vic Your mother was crying. Doris was crying. I was crying. I'd never seen anything like it, all that pomp and circumstance.

John It's a load of old rubbish.

Vic I said to your mother, when I'd sat down, 'I think we'll go away. I think we'll go abroad.'

Liz Always fancied Greece, I did.

Vic   Spain. That's what she said. She said she'd always wanted to go to Torremolinos.

John   Go to Paris.

Vic   Can't speak it.

John   But you can't speak Spanish.

Vic   No, but they speak English; the French don't like us.

John   Learn French.

Vic   Me? No, I'm too old.

John   Go to night school. Do something, Dad, you're not stupid, you're bright. Don't wallow in it. Do sommat different. Re-train, you're young enough. Run a night class for jokes.

Vic   *Comedians.*

John   Unquestionably.

Vic   No, I knew when they merged areas there'd be redundancies. And there's millions of tons of coal to dig. They don't need me. Besides I use all my mental skills keeping up with your mother.

Liz   She should never have had them dogs. They killed you. You tired yourself out with them dogs.

Jack   They're good dogs.

Liz   They made her house stink.

John   I'll buy you a tape; you can learn French.

Liz   She lets them sleep at the bottom of the bed.

Vic   No, I'm not learning any other language.

John   (*nastily*)   Well, waste away then.

Vic   (*warningly*)   Not today, please not today. Let's just have one day without any arguments.

Liz They had separate beds; what sort of a marriage was that?

Vic When we pulled up at the university my heart was beating. All those old buildings, all that brain power. I felt really small, you know. Really small. And then that car pulls up at the side of mine. A Rolls, wasn't it?

John A Bentley.

Vic And I could see them look down their noses at us. They looked at us and they thought, 'Oh, look at that, they've only got a Hillman Minx.' And then when it came to it she only had a pass degree; I looked down the booklet and she only had a pass.

John They're nice people, Dad.

Vic And she's looking at us like they think they're it, and she only had a pass. I could see 'em looking at my cheap suit and thinking.

Liz I could have done with separate beds with you.

Jack Ar.

Liz You did nothing but kick. You'd twitch and then kick me; I used to kick you back.

Vic A second-hand Hillman'll do for me.

Jack I was asleep, didn't know I was doing it.

Liz Kick, kick.

Liz *and* **Jack** *exit.*

John Where's my Mam?

Vic She's sweeping down the path. She's got a job working for the council.

John Funny.

Vic He was a doctor, him in the Bentley. He had

'Doctor on Call' in his windscreen. And I've worked at
the pit all that time, dreaming of sommat happening
for you. That's why I stood up and clapped.

Dot *and* **Doris** *enter. Both are smartly dressed;* **Dot** *is
wearing* **John**'s *academic gown and cap over her own clothes.
They are behaving very girlishly.*

Dot   That's about it, that should do it.

Vic   That's why I stood up and clapped.

Dot (*referring to the cap and gown*)   I think the whole
street should have seen it; I've swept all the way down
to Rattigan's.

John   Oh, no.

Dot   I feel very good in it. I might get one.

Vic   Have you been sweeping up in that?

Dot   Course I have.

John   You're an embarrassment.

Dot   No, I'm not.

Doris   We're only having a laugh. I've had it on. I
felt really intelligent, didn't I, nip?

Dot   She's had it on.

Doris   I have. I thought, I'm having a go with that,
see if any brains rub off.

Dot   She's been running around the garden in it.

Vic   I bet she looked like a bloody witch.

Doris   I came out with a long word. Mississippi.
Didn't I, nip?

Dot   That's a long word.

Vic   Elastic, that's a long word.

John   Please?

Vic   It stretches.

John   You're all embarrassing.

Dot   Don't be so touchy.

John   Well you are. Jesus Christ.

Dot   We're just family having fun. And stop swearing.

Doris   Don't spoil it.

Vic (*angrily*)   He always does.

John (*to* **Dot**)   She's embarrassing.

Dot   She?

Liz *enters.*

Liz   She's the cat's mother. (*She sits.*)

Doris   She's the cat's mother is what my Mam'd say.

John   I don't believe you lot. Just tell me this: is there a history of mental ill-health in this family? I'll keep an eye out for the symptoms. I mean my grandad's dad might have been a madman.

Doris   Don't be so sensitive.

John   It's her, my mother. She's round the bend. She tells everybody our business.

Dot   I don't.

John   She told that woman in the office my life history and we only went to ask her where to park.

Dot   I didn't.

Vic   He'll spoil it.

John   You'll have to learn to keep your mouth shut when I'm with other people, Mother.

Dot   Why?

John   Because they don't want to hear you come out

with a load of old bloody rubbish. I was talking to the head of the Education faculty about something and my mother came up to me and asked me if I'd had a shave.

Dot Had you?

John Don't be funny, Mother. It dun't suit yer.

Dot Well, it didn't look like you had to me.

John The poor bloke didn't know where to look.

Vic Well, if he couldn't deal with that he shouldn't be in education.

John Dad, that's not the point.

Dot All right, then, know-all, what else have I done?

Liz She'll never let go of him.

John The whole day was awful.

Doris I thought it was lovely.

John I wanted to die. My mother asked the Bursar's wife if her two-piece was from Marks and Spencer's.

Dot I was making conversation.

Doris It was a lovely two-piece she had on.

Dot It wasn't from Marks. She said it was, but it wasn't.

Vic She's a Marksist, your mother, John.

John I should have left home and never come back.

Doris He should have had a shave.

John I'll tell you this, I'm never coming home again. I can't stand it.

Dot Did you see her hair?

Doris Awful, wasn't it?

Vic (*to* **John**) It was your idea for your mother to put the gown on. You were the one who was embarrassing. You thought it was funny.

John I wasn't the one who was shouting 'He's doing an MA' at the top of my voice, was I?

Doris I heard that.

Vic She's proud.

Dot I got talking to this woman and then some others came out onto the grass and they were talking loud. And she was all snooty.

Doris Which one was she, nip?

Dot Her in that C&A print.

Doris I thought that was awful. Didn't suit her.

Dot She just came up to me and told me that her daughter had got a teaching job in Bath.

Vic I saw her, she came and told me.

John She told everybody.

Doris Reminded me of your Edna.

Vic *She* was embarrassing.

John Yes, but she wasn't *my* mother.

Dot And she kept going on about this teaching job and how many hadn't got jobs, and she says, 'Has he got a job?' So I says, 'No.'

Vic Playing her along?

Dot Like you do. . . . No, I says, he hasn't got a job. 'Oh that's a shame, but it's hard.' And then I said, 'He's going to do an MA.'

Doris I heard that.

Dot But she didn't hear, so I shouted it to her.

Vic   Her face dropped a foot. Everybody looked over.

Doris   You could have stood on her lower lip.

John   But she shouldn't have told them!

Vic   Why?

John   Because I'm embarrassed because I can pay. Because I've got to pay. . . . My grandad slogged his bloody soul-case out and left me eight hundred pounds. Three others from our college had applied. We'd all been offered places. None of us had got a grant. And that money is taking me out of here and I'm not like you. You've pushed me away and I can never come back. (*He indicates his head.*) I've left you, up here. I'm Rebecca now, that's what I am; I'm a Martian. And it just goes on. The gap getting bigger and bigger and bigger, until there's just nothingness, silence. And I love you, Christ I love you, but it does me in.

Dot   Stop that.

John (*exasperated*)   Oh Jesus.

Vic   We've always known that you'd go. You have to go. Me and your mam have always known that you wouldn't stay here. What did you think we wanted for you?

John   I don't know, Dad.

Vic   Whatever we did we did for you. We never did you any harm.

John   Not much. I didn't know what sex was until I was nineteen. Whenever the subject came up here, me mam coughed and you made yourself a coffee. No wonder we're all 'fucked up', and don't worry, I'm quoting. It's safe, I'm quoting.

Vic   Mis-quoting. I read books and all. (*He pauses.*) You don't have to go to college, kid, to read books.

John   Where are we going as a family, Dad? Where are we going?

There is a silence.

Vic   I don't know; I just don't understand you. You had to spoil today, didn't you?

There is another silence. Everyone looks uncomfortable.

Dot   I'll make some tea, shall I?

Doris   Oh, lovely. I'm dying for a cuppa. I thought we'd be able to have a cup when we were there but the spread was very poor. Wasn't it a poor spread, Vic?

Vic   It was, Doris. It was, yes.

Dot   Do you want a drink, kid. Earl Grey?

John (*lightly*)   I don't know why I bother trying to explain. . . . Yes, yes . . . I'll have a cuppa Earl Grey.

There is a silence.

Dot   I'll make some tea and then we'll have a bit of a bite.

Vic   I could eat a horse.

Doris   I'm a bit peckish. Are you, kid, are you peckish?

John   I am a bit, yeah. I'm peckish.

Liz   He should be allowed to do what he wants with his life.

Vic   I stood up and clapped. I must be going around the bend. Stood up and clapped.

Doris   We could have a game after tea. We could play Scrabble. Who wants a game of Scrabble?

Liz   He stood up and clapped.

Jack He's as soft as a brush.

Dot I wish your Edna could have come.

Vic She sent a card. It's a nice card.

Dot I wish they ... well, you know ... I'm not upsetting myself ... (*But of course she is.*)

John I'll play Scrabble on condition that you don't cheat, Aunty Doris.

Doris I don't cheat.

John Not much. You're like my dad – you make words up. What was the last one? It was a classic.

Vic Clapter.

John That's it, clapter.

Doris It's a word. Clapter. It's what an audience does at the end of a play.

John She means applause.

Doris Clapter, like laughter. 'There was a lot of clapter.'

John I'm not playing with her, she cheats.

There is a pause.

Doris (*softly*) I don't.

Dot Our Doris is crackers.

Liz She's all right, she is.

Vic Bloody clapter?

Doris (*remembering*) Oh, I don't know. We've had some laughs.

There is another pause.

Dot Can you remember when she sat in the garden?

Vic I can.

Dot   It was that summer your Edna was here. Can you remember? Rebecca had just got a first and Vic was going on about it. I knew then he'd get a first . . . I knew it.

Doris   I can remember. (*She sits on the arm of the sofa.*)

Vic   The good old days, eh, Doris?

Dot   I knew he'd get a first.

John   I didn't get a first though, Mam, I got a two-one.

Dot   I'll put the kettle on.

Vic (*easily*)   It'll not fit you.

Dot *takes off the gown and hands it to* **Doris**. **John** *sits on the sofa.*

Dot   Here, you'd better have this or I'll be cleaning up in it.

John   That's another thing, isn't it? I was the only one in my group who bought his cap and gown.

Vic   Well, we didn't know you could hire 'em.

Doris   It's a once in a lifetime thing, isn't it?

Vic   Course it is.

Doris   Here, I'll have it if you don't want it; I can make some curtains.

Dot (*becoming very emotional*)   I wish, you know . . .

Vic (*comforting*)   Don't set yourself off.

The lights change. **Dot**, **Doris** *and* **Vic** *freeze.* **John** *moves from the sofa to an armchair. He addresses the audience.*

John   That was the last time I spent summer at home. We sat in the garden and everyone took turns in trying on my cap and gown. It was also the last time I saw my gran and grandad so clearly in my head; I don't hear them as often now, and as time has gone by I've almost forgotten what they looked like. I'm not even certain of how much I've told you is the truth. Our memory plays such tricks. But I did get an MA and the only teaching job I could get was at the comprehensive down the road. So I start teaching Drama on Monday.

The lights change. **John** *sits in the armchair. The rest of the cast comes out of the freeze.* **Dot** *is very upset.*

Dot   They would have been proud.

Doris   Yeah.

Dot   Anyway.

Liz   Is she putting that kettle on or what?

Liz *exits. There is a silence.*

Vic   Anyway.

Dot   I can just see my mother's face; she would have been having a little titter to herself.

Doris   Yeah, she would.

Dot (*crying*)   I miss 'em . . .

Doris *stands and comforts her sister.*

Dot   I miss 'em . . .

Doris   Yeah . . .

There is a silence.

Vic (*breaking the sombre mood deliberately*)   So what is there to eat, buggerlugs? I'm starving.

Dot (*steeling herself emotionally*)   Why, what do you fancy, Horse Teeth?

Vic   I just fancy getting me teeth into a slice of tinned ham.

Dot (*happily*)   Oh ... you little devil ...

Frank Sinatra singing 'You Make Me Feel So Young' plays.
Dot, **Doris** *and* **Vic** *exit, leaving the cap and gown draped over the sofa.* **John** *is left alone, sitting in the armchair. The lights slowly fade to black.*

Curtain.

Shakers
Restirred

Shakers was first presented by Hull Truck Theatre Company at the Spring Street Theatre, Hull, on 29 January 1984, with the following cast:

Adele	Alison Grant
Carol	Alison Watt
Mel	Marion Summerfield
Nicky	Sherry Baines

Directed by John Godber

Shakers Restirred was first presented by the Hull Truck Theatre Company in 1991, with the following cast:

Adele	Nicola Vickery
Carol	Joanne Wootton
Mel	Tracy Sweetinburgh
Nicky	Rebecca Clay

Directed by John Godber
Designed by Liam Doona

Act One

*A modern café bar, post-modernist structure, which is essentially
an open space. Four chairs are the only real furniture. Four girls
are dressed in the height of fashion. They are waitresses. Lights
rise. They stand centre stage and are lit by spotlight.*

Adele Ladies and gentlemen welcome to Shakers.
That trendy bar in the main street where the neon
light shines out into the night tempting passers-by.
That place where dreams come true. Where time
stands still, where everyone wants to be seen, from the
checkout girls to the chinless yuppies . . .

Carol
 Where *pied à terre* hs replaced Hush Puppies.
 Where the plastic world has taken root,
 And the social climber counts his loot . . .

Mel
 We stand and serve, we grin and smile,
 We serve to please, and all the while
 We do, we burn up deep inside
 With all the pain we're meant to hide.

Nicky
 And though at times we'd like to scream,
 It wouldn't wake you from your dream
 Of Long Tall Ice and deep-freeze beer.
 We see you glance, we know you leer . . .

Adele
 And secretly you long to touch us as we pass.
 And rub your hands across our arse,
 And wink and smile and glow with lust.
 We work this bar that is worse than hell.

Carol We are Carol.

Adele Adele.

Nicky   Nicky.

Mel   And Mel.

Adele
We pull the drinks,
We take your bile,
We serve the food . . .

Mel
We have to smile
No matter how crude or rude you care to be.

Carol
No matter what you do . . .

Nicky
No matter what you say . . .

Adele
There's a happy smiling face that comes your way.

Lights up, we are in 'real' mode. The girls clean. The bar is about to open. **Carol** *addresses the audience.*

Carol   I'm sorry, we're closed, you'll have to come back later. Sorry.

Mel   Time is it?

Nicky   Quarter to.

Mel   Another day another dollar . . .

Carol   Closed, read the sign.

Mel   If you can read.

Nicky   Happy hour doesn't start till seven. That's when all the fun starts.

Carol   Yippee!

Nicky   Happy hour, seven till ten.

Mel   It's a long hour.

Nicky   And not very happy.

Adele   ... It can be desperate.

Nicky   That'd make a change, 'desperate hour' seven till ten, bring your own Valium.

Carol   Some of the people we get in here you need it.

Adele   Valium?

Mel (*to audience*)   We are closed, come back in ten minutes, we're having a chat so knob off!

Adele   A true professional at work.

Carol   Charming.

Mel   That's how to deal with 'em. They think we're shit, I think they're shit, I don't take any prisoners.

Nicky   No ... they'd rather kill themselves I'll bet.

Carol   I just ignore the awkward ones.

Adele   Sensible.

Mel   Well you must ignore everybody in that case Carol, you must be the only waitress in here who doesn't serve anybody. They're all a set of bastards.

Carol   Thank you Desmond Morris.

Nicky   Who?

Mel   This is the real world, Carol.

Carol   Don't start that again.

Mel   This is the real world, mad bad and ugly.

Nicky   Like you ...

Mel   Go and die Nicky, OK.

Carol   This is the real world is it?

Adele   'Fraid so.

Mel   What time did you get in Adele? I didn't notice.

Adele   You what?

Mel   What time did you get in?

Adele   When?

Mel   Tonight.

Adele   Why?

Mel   I just wondered.

Adele   Listen Mel I'm here, that's the important thing.

Nicky   True enough.

Adele   I'll never let you down, that's the important thing.

Carol   Go on then Mel.

Mel   What?

Carol   I thought you were going to tell us something.

Mel   Who?

Carol   You. You couldn't contain yourself about half an hour ago and now you've gone all shy on us.

Nicky   That's not like you.

Mel   Oh it is, I'm very shy and retiring I am. All the family are.

Carol   Do you mean there's more like you?

Adele   Go on then.

Mel   What?

Nicky   Tell us . . .

Mel   He's asked me.

Carol   Who?

Mel   Steve.

Nicky   You hardly know him.

Adele   I thought it was Paul?

Nicky   That was last month.

Mel   Ha ha.

Carol   So it's the real thing?

Adele   So is Coke.

Nicky   But it rots your teeth.

Mel   At least I've got a bloke Carol . . .

Carol   Yeah . . . lucky you.

Nicky   Will it last though, that's what we all want to know?

Mel   I hope.

Nicky   How long have you known him?

Mel   Long enough.

Adele   How long is that?

Mel   How long do you want it to be?

Nicky   Oooohhhh

Mel   What's up Adele, are you jealous?

Adele   Yeah jealous to death.

Mel   I bet you are and all.

Nicky   What's happened to Paul then? He looked nice. He'd be alright for me. I like spotty men.

Mel   I think Paul fancied Adele actually.

Adele   I'm flattered.

Mel   But I think he got scared off.

Nicky   But not as frightening as Paul, I should know I saw him in the daylight.

Carol   He wasn't that bad.

Mel   Yes he was.

Adele   When's the big day Mel?

Mel   Soon.

Nicky   Is it going to be in peach . . . or lemon?

Mel   Lemon I think. You'll all get an invite. And you can bring a man each. If you can find one.

Nicky   You could have Emma as a bridesmaid.

Adele   I don't think so.

Mel   Where do you leave her?

Adele   I usually leave her with my mum. But my mum's ill. So I've left her with Craig's mum, tonight.

Mel   Oh right.

Adele   Congratulations.

Mel   Thanks.

Adele   I hope you're as happy as I thought I was going to be.

Mel   I'm sure I will be.

Nicky   I wish I could find the real thing in my life.

Carol   Why?

Nicky   All the men I meet are like cartoon characters.

Adele   There are plenty of fish in the sea.

Nicky   That's what I thought.

Mel   Yeah but she's not looking for a fish are you?

Nicky I don't know what I'm looking for. All that can wait anyway, I've had some good news today, so the world is my oyster.

Carol Speaking of which . . .

Adele The seafood pasta is back on.

Carol There's a taste of class . . .

Nicky In a highball glass. Cocktails on ice.

Mel You want a lemon slice?

Adele Or a Piña Colada?

Carol Or a Vodka Hula?

Nicky Tequila Sunrise?

Mel Or a Southern Gin Cooler?

Carol It looks exciting.

Mel It looks a scream.

Adele But you pay through the nose, when your head's in a dream.

They move to next positions. **Nicky** *and* **Carol** *become two punters, Daz and Trev.*

Nicky Daz.

Carol And Trev . . .

Adele Hard as nails . . .

Carol They shop at Next . . .

Mel And have been in jail . . .

Carol They're out on the town . . .

Adele They're after the skirt . . .

Carol It's fifteen below . . .

Nicky It's freezing out there . . . but these lads are hard.

Mel   They don't give a toss.

Nicky   They've got muscles like knots, in dental floss
... they're Daz ...

Carol   And they're Trev ...

Nicky   They've come down to the bar ...

Carol   To get themselves a bev ...

Nicky   Go on then Trev ask her.

Carol   You ask her.

Nicky   What's wrong are you scared? Chicken shit.

Carol   I don't want a farty cocktail anyway, I'd
rather have a pint.

Nicky   It'll be a laugh, see her face.

Carol   OK, which one are you going to ask?

Nicky   The one with the tits, not that other one,
she's too skinny.

Carol   Yeah that big one's alright.

Nicky   Yeah not many of them to a pound.

Carol   You're well hard.

Nicky   Too right.

Carol   How much are they?

Nicky   I don't think they're for sale.

Carol   I meant the drinks dickhead.

Nicky   About two quid, I think.

Carol   It's not worth it.

Nicky   Course it is, for a laugh.

Carol   Loads of blokes'll ask her for it, I bet she

doesn't bat an eyelid.

Nicky Yes but are they good-looking?

Carol Like you, you mean?

Nicky You said it mate.

Carol Look out she's coming over.

Nicky Brilliant.

Mel *arrives to serve them.*

Mel Are you being served?

Carol No we're not.

Mel Can I help you?

Carol Yes, he wants one of them cocktails.

Mel Which one do you fancy?

Nicky They both look alright to me darling. No offence.

They both laugh.

Carol Excuse my friend, he doesn't know how to behave in front of ladies.

Mel Really?

Carol Yes.

Mel I had noticed.

Nicky I want a Long Slow Comfortable Screw. So how about that?

Mel What a surprise. Regular or giant-sized?

Nicky You what?

Mel Large or small?

Nicky Don't get personal.

Carol You guess love.

Nicky   Make a wish. (*They laugh.*)

Carol   Sorry love just a joke.

Mel   Oh, is that what it was?

Nicky   Yeah, funny eh?

Mel   Very.

Carol   Don't smile much do you?

Nicky   Too much bed, not enough sleep, eh?

Mel   Look do you want a drink or not, I haven't got all night.

Nicky   How much are they?

Mel   Three quid for a small one seven quid for a large one.

Nicky   What a rip-off.

Carol   Expensive in't it?

Mel   You don't have to have one.

Nicky   Don't get touchy.

Mel   I'm waiting.

Carol   She's waiting.

Nicky   I'll have a small one.

Carol   And me.

Mel   With or without ice?

Both   Erm, with ice . . .

Mel   Bleeding cocktails, it's the same every night. You always get a couple of uptown Zombies with a Glad Eye doing a Pick Me Up, sometimes promising a holiday with a Tequila Sunrise on Montego Bay, hoping for a ride on his Piña Colada. What he really wants is a Long Slow Comfortable Screw, Between the

Sheets in his Side Car. I'd just like to give the Bosom Caresser a Sparkling Punch in his Dicki Dicki, so he falls Head over Heels and goes home clutching his Blue Bols. Six pounds please.

The actresses pick up the serving rhythm and move around the stage.

Carol   You want a Piña Colada?

Nicky   Or a Vodka Hula?

Carol   Tequila Sunrise?

Mel   Or a Southern Gin Cooler?

Adele   Whatever you ask for we can make. Just give us a name and we'll give you a shake.

Mel   I've just served two right prats.

Adele   What's new?

Mel   Not a lot actually.

Adele   We can have a breather before the rush starts. I hate Fridays.

Mel   And Mondays, Tuesdays, Wednesdays.

Adele (*to* **Mel**)   You're really funny.

Nicky   I don't mind Fridays. I mean at least it's busy and you don't have to stand about like a spare part. I like it like that, makes it seem more worthwhile.

Carol   And Mario gets more value for money.

Nicky   And the time passes quicker. It's better than doing nothing.

Mel   Is it?

Nicky   I think it is.

Mel   I'd rather do nothing. You get paid the same.

We could sit at the bar all night, put the stereo on, have a chat . . . that'd be great.

Adele   I don't think I'd bother coming.

Mel   I'm not saying anything Adele.

Adele   Razor-sharp tonight aren't you?

Nicky   My feet are killing me already.

Adele   So who have we got in tonight?

Mel   I'm surprised you're even interested.

Carol   There's a theatre booking. And a twenty-first birthday party coming in at nine.

Mel   Oh nice, all streamers and funny hats?

Carol   And the usual crowd.

Nicky   Oh don't be like that Mel, they've probably been looking forward to this all day.

Music, 'The Girl from Ipanema'. **Mel**, **Nicky**, **Carol** *and* **Adele** *become Susan, Elaine, Sharon and Tracey, respectively. They all work at the supermarket and are set at the checkout tills. It's quiet in terms of customers. Muzak plays.*

All   'Supermarket.'

Nicky   Cheque for fifty. (*Pounds.*)

Mel   Susan.

Nicky   Elaine: twenty-one and should be celebrating.

All   Yeahhhhhh . . . (*A cheer that tails off.*)

Carol   Tracey.

Adele   Sharon.

Nicky   God it's dragging.

Mel   I'm bored.

Adele I'm vegetating . . .

Carol I hate it on the tills, me. In the last half hour all I've had is an old woman with some organic tomatoes.

Adele It's always the same this time of day.

Mel Yeah, boring.

Carol I was supposed to be on the shop floor today doing cereals, but they've put that bloody student on, it makes me sick.

Nicky It's not fair is it?

Carol I mean, she's only here for the holidays. I don't like her.

Adele No, I don't.

Carol I wouldn't care but I was loading bloody freezers all day yesterday, my hands nearly dropped off it was that cold.

Mel They should give you gloves you know. You're not supposed to do it without gloves.

Carol I know.

Mel But they don't care.

Carol No. (*Pause.*)

Nicky What a birthday . . .

Adele Never mind.

Nicky I can't wait for tonight.

Mel Yeah, at least that's something to look forward to.

Carol I can't believe you're twenty-one . . .

Nicky Well I am . . .

Carol But it seems so old.

Adele   It's not exactly middle aged. You've got your whole life ahead.

Nicky   Yeah, and I'll tell you what, I might pack it in here, I might do that hairdressing course at tech that our Sandra's doing. She says it's great.

Carol   You wouldn't have as much money though would you?

Nicky   Who's bothered? I've always fancied hairdressing, and it's got to be better than this.

Carol   I suppose so.

Nicky   Our Sandra's doing my hair for when we go out.

Adele   Oh yes?

Nicky   French plait.

Mel   Oh.

Adele   What are you wearing?

Mel   That black dress again I suppose.

Carol   It's nice that.

Mel   It's alright.

Nicky   Me, Shaz and Trace are off shopping at dinner time for some new stuff.

Mel   God . . .

Nicky   Well it is my twenty-first.

Adele   You can come if you want.

Mel   I can't, I've got no money.

Adele   There's a sale on.

Mel   Oh go on then . . .

Carol   We need something smart, it's posh that

Shakers place you know.

Nicky Now that's something I wouldn't mind.

All What?

Nicky Working in a cocktail bar!

Music to take us back into Shakers. The girls become the waitresses. They meet around centre stage.

Nicky I think I've got a corn.

Adele Yeah table four. The man with the horse teeth and the B. O.

Carol That's right. Sweetcorn, two tagliatelles and a bottle of house red.

Nicky No, on my foot.

Carol Stop wingeing.

Mel Have you seen that bloke with the nose and the glasses?

Nicky Have I? He's been dying to ask me for a Slow Screw, I can see him looking at it on the menu, then he comes to the bar all determined, and he chickens out and asked for Aqua Libra and some peanuts.

Carol Good job by the looks of him.

Nicky I can't understand it, he still blushes.

Adele He looks nice.

Mel Well with them peanuts and that chilli pizza he'll pebble-dash the toilets.

Nicky Ugh, Mel.

Mel Well he will. Pebble-dash man, or what?

Adele As long as we don't have to clear it away.

Mel Are you coming tomorrow Adele?

Adele   Why?

Mel   Just asking that's all . . .

Adele   Don't worry Mel.

Mel   It's just that it's not fair on us, we have to set up. I mean we haven't told Mario you were late.

Adele   Yet?

The four actresses react to the last line with a loud guffaw of laughter. They have instantly become businessmen.

Mel   A table for three love, a table for three.

Nicky   Here we go . . .

Mel   No it's alright we'll stand at the bar.

Nicky   Certainly.

Mel   Is that alright, Gerry? Mervyn?

Carol   Gerry . . .

Adele   Mervyn . . .

Mel   Yes that's tickety boo . . . Stand at the bar, prevent anyone else being served . . .

A guffaw of laughter from the businessmen.

Nicky   Can I get you a drink? It's Happy Hour at the moment. Double measures for the price of one.

Mel   Amazing.

Carol   Absolutely.

Adele   Of course.

Mel   What do you have?

Nicky   What would you like, sir?

Mel   Too early for any of that thank you.

Carol   Speak for yourself.

Mel   I was. (*A loud laugh.*)

Nicky   Sorry.

Mel   You would be . . .

Nicky   You wait for hours until the fat oaf has decided what he wants. Then, after adjusting his trousers several times, he'll go for the lager.

Mel   I'll have a lager.

Nicky   Then he'll suddenly change his mind, because of his blood pressure.

Mel   No no no . . . must think about the old blood pressure.

Nicky   And you nod, like you're concerned.

Mel   I think I'll have . . .

Nicky   He'll go for the Martini.

Mel   Martini.

Nicky   Knew it. With lemonade and ice.

Mel   With . . .

Nicky   Lemonade and ice, sir?

Mel   How marvellous. What's everyone else having, Gerry? Mervyn? What's your poison?

Nicky   They've just been looking at a new car outside.

Adele   We've just been looking at a new car outside.

Mel   What're you having?

Adele   Martini.

Carol   And me, Willy.

Mel   Three Martinis lovey . . .

Nicky   I wince and smile . . . and serve . . .

They take the drinks and down-the-hatch. It takes their breath.

Carol Wonderful.

Mel Excellent.

Adele Didn't even touch the sides.

Mel Same again Gerry? Mervyn?

Carol Gerry.

Adele Mervyn.

Carol Oh I don't know.

Adele I have a hell of a drive.

Carol Oh what the hell . . .

Nicky And four doubles later the laughter starts . . .

All laugh loud and hard.

Adele This man goes into a butcher's, and he says to the butcher. 'Have you got a sheep's head?' And the butcher says, 'No, it's just the way I comb my hair.'

Mel Bloody hell, that's bloody funny . . .

Carol I say Willy, what are you driving at the moment?

Mel Me . . . a car . . . (*All guffaw.*) No but seriously I'm driving the new Sierra.

Carol Really, how do you find it?

Mel Well I just open the garage door and there it is . . .

Carol Nice girl . . . the waitress, nice legs.

Adele Yes she reminds me of Jackie at the office.

Mel Which one's Jackie?

Adele Tall brunette with the dirty mouth.

Mel Oh yes rather. Whenever she comes into my office I ask her to take something down.

Carol . . . But she never does . . .

Mel Well she hasn't done yet. (*Laughter.*)

Adele Aren't they awkward on the road?

Mel More awkward in the cupboard.

Adele I meant the Sierra, more's the pity.

Mel No no, they're fine.

Adele I'm still with the old Rover.

Carol Yes, how is Vicky, Willy?

Mel Shit Vicky, must ring the old girl . . . (*Phones.*) Hello Vicky, it's Willy. Hello darling how are you? Really? So sorry. Look, I know we're meeting Glenys and Clive but I'm afraid I'm still at the office, yes, something's come up . . . I'll try to get back later darling. But it's hell here at the moment . . . Love you, bye. Vicky is just the most amazing woman in the world.

Carol Does she know about you and . . .

Mel Of course not. Anyway me and Becky are only having a bit of fun. She's married as well, her husband is in accounts.

Adele Bloody hell Willy, a bit near home.

Carol Oh look at the pissing time chaps, another drink whilst it's reasonable?

Adele I'd say the same again . . .

Mel Cigar?

All Cheers.

Mel I say, would anyone care to eat?

Adele   But what about Vicky's meal?

Mel   Oh it'll keep. Have you tasted Vicky's food? It's like bloody rubber.

Carol   Well I could deal with a snack.

Mel   I say . . . lovey, can we have a table for three, we've decided we'd like to eat.

Nicky   Certainly sir, where would you like to sit?

Mel   On your face . . . (*A loud guffaw.*)

Nicky   Your table is ready, sir . . .

Mel   I'm sorry?

Nicky   Your table is ready . . . Fatty.

Mel   Excellent. Another drink anyone . . .

Carol   Gerry?

Adele   Mervyn?

Mel   And can we have the wine list?

Nicky   Of course . . . you silly old farts. (*They become the girls.*)

Mel   There's an arse-pincher. Table ten, by the bogs.

Adele   Lucky you.

Mel   Just be aware.

Carol   They should be locked up.

Nicky   The fat bloke on table six is having an affair and his wife can't cook.

Adele   That's why he's having the affair.

Mel   Well have a good look at the arse-pincher on ten, I'm sure he's wearing a wig . . .

The girls are serving imaginary characters, calling orders and receiving orders in turn, and also commenting on the evening so far.

Carol   One minestrone.

Nicky   One onion soup?

Adele   It's full already.

Carol   Packed.

Adele   Seafood pasta?

Mel   That is definitely a wig. He's bald as a bastard.

Nicky   It's not a wig ... Anyone order the garlic bread?

Adele   Put the air-conditioning on.

Mel   It's knackered.

Adele   Great stuff. It is, it's a wig.

Carol   One minestrone?

Nicky   It's like being on a tube.

Carol   Excuse me, coming through.

Adele   Sorry?

Mel   Well why don't you move then? Thank you Adele I told you it was. I can spot 'em a mile off.

Adele   Anyone ordered seafood pasta?

Nicky   Oh God these shoes.

Carol   What?

Nicky   Can you hear me?

Adele   THE MUSIC IS TOO LOUD.

Carol   You what?

Nicky   Shout up!

Carol (*shouts*)   Is it a wig? Or what?

Nicky What about that, he's not going back to his wife, he's going to meet Becky. It's all go.

Carol Onion soup?

Adele Prawn cocktail?

Mel Sweetcorn?

Nicky Excuse me, coming through, mind your backs please. Gerry's going to cover for him.

Carol Mind the doors.

Adele Mind the yuppies.

Nicky Mind the liars.

Adele *steps centre. This allows the others to peel away and set up the next tableaux.*

Adele It's like a madhouse, cocktails then food, food then cocktails, I don't know if I'm coming or going. I don't know my Tom Collins from my Bolognese. Craig's mum's great she is, but I don't like leaving my little girl with her ... I mean tonight ... I don't know my head from my arse. I nearly had a stroke getting here, I was charging down the street like somebody not right.

Nicky *has become a yuppie woman,* **Mel** *and* **Carol** *serve upstage in a freeze.*

Nicky Excuse me, you.

Adele Me?

Nicky Yes.

Adele Oh God here we go.

Nicky I'll take a mineral water with a lemon twist.

Adele Of course.

Nicky With ice ...

Adele (*to audience*)   She obviously thinks I'm a dog.
Bastard.

Nicky   Sorry?

Adele   Badoit?

Nicky   Evian.

Adele   Woof woof...

As **Adele** *crosses the stage,* **Carol***, as a yuppie man, grabs
and fondles her arse. It's almost erotic.*

Adele   Get off.

Carol   What's wrong ... I was just trying to get past
you.

Nicky   I saw that Carl, you bastard...

Carol   Vicky they love it, it's what they look forward
to, someone to brighten up the evening for them.
Marry me ... marry me ...

Nicky   Never ... (*She breaks away from the scene and
explains briefly to the audience.*) I don't need to, I'm young,
a successful interior designer, I have toe-capped shoes
and a mobile phone, I was educated at a top people's
finishing school, and I also have a beautiful daughter
with whom I can afford to spend quality time ...

Carol   Vicky you are an amazing woman.

Nicky   And a very rich father in the City.

Carol   I love the City.

Mel *becomes an outraged punter. Screaming, shouting at*
Adele*.*

Mel   You you you ...

Carol (*Carl*)   Can I make an order?

Mel   You ... you.

Adele   Me?

Mel   I haven't had my soup.

Adele   It's on its way.

Nicky   Where's my Evian . . . ?

Carol   Can I make an order now . . . ?

Mel   Am I going to get served in here tonight or not?

Adele   It's on its way.

Mel   We should have gone to Alexander's . . .

Nicky   You.

Carol   You.

Nicky   Oh come on . . .

Carol   Can we have some pissing service . . .

Nicky   This is ridiculous.

A slow motion sequence. **Adele** *is bringing* **Nicky** *her drink, she slips on the floor. The drink flies into the air and then spills all over* **Nicky** *and* **Carol** *(Carl.)*

Nicky   Oh oh oh my God, oh my God . . .

Adele   Oh sorry sorry . . . I'm . . .

Nicky   This cost me six hundred pounds at Katherine Hamnet.

Adele   Sorry Katherine. Sorry.

Nicky   Seafood pasta.

The waitresses are involved in chaotic serving.

Mel   Did you do that on purpose?

Adele   . . . No it was an accident.

Mel   You bloody liar . . .

Nicky   Seafood pasta?

Carol I'm sure you ordered sirloin.

Adele . . . Another Lambrusco.

Mel Another round of garlic mushrooms?

Nicky (*shouts*) Has any one ordered seafood bloody pasta?

Adele (*a punter*) Do you have any black pepper?

Mel Excuse me this wine is corked.

Adele This lager is off.

Nicky One seafood pasta going back into the sea.

Carol I'm coming through watch your backs please.

Mel (*a punter*) This wine is corked.

Adele Would madam like a kick in the teeth now or would she prefer it with her liqueur?

Nicky *downstage, with the others acting as chorus.* NB: '**All**' *denotes all except* **Nicky**.

Nicky At eight o'clock the theatre lot have gone to watch the curtain-up

Carol The mobile phones are up and off, and the power dressers disappear, talking of their business stresses.

Adele
And it must be said there's no respite.
This time of night, from the obtuse abuse,
From the suited bods, the boring sods.

Mel
And they're here too, the local hacks,
And the yuppies with their Filofax,
Who pinch your arse and laugh.

All Ha ha.

Mel
  They all have their tale to tell,
  Arse-pinching yuppies who come from hell.

Carol
  And at this time the tips are few
  And the basic manners, too.

Adele *breaks into a loud-mouthed man.*

Adele   Excuse me, am I going to have to sit here and eat this rancid sirloin with my blessed fingers?

Carol   Sorry sir. It's on its way.

Adele   I should think so, I'll never eat in here again. And furthermore I'll recommend to all my very influential, and red-faced friends that they avoid the place like the plague. Stupid girl.

Carol   I'm not stupid. (*All four become waitresses.*)

Mel   Mario's sent him a bottle of champagne.

Nicky   Greasy bastard.

Carol   That's calmed him down.

Adele   Yeah I know, he's even left a tip.

Carol   How much?

Mel   Nosey.

Adele   And off into the night he farts, a big, bloated balloon of Beaujolais, following his stomach the way a navvy follows a wheelbarrow.

Nicky   Having left a pound coin he feels sexy about himself.

Adele   Good night, sir.

Mel   Don't Adele. I hate men . . . like that.

Adele   He disappears into the night, a large Sierra, a magistrate.

Carol   Ignorant bastard.

Nicky   Carol?

Adele   He might have problems at home.

Mel   Yeah I bet.

Carol (*the lights begin to fade to a spotlight on* **Carol**)   I can't help it, I hate it when people just assume that because you do a job like this, you're thick. You know there's some nights I just can't stand it, I can't. I want to stand up on top of the bar and shout: 'I've got "O" levels, and I've got "A" levels and a Bachelor of Arts degree. So don't condescend to me, don't pretend you feel sorry for me and don't treat me like I can't read or talk or join in any of your conversations because I can.' I see these teenage-like men and women with their well-cut suits and metal briefcases, discussing the City and the arts and time-shares in Tuscany, and I'm jealous, because I can't work out how they've achieved that success. It's so difficult. You see I want to be a photographer, take portraits. I won a competition in a magazine. It was this photo of a punk sat in a field on an old discarded toilet. It was brilliant. Anyway, after college I had this wonderful idea that I'd go to London with my portfolio. I was confident that I'd get loads of work. But it wasn't like that. The pictures were great they said, but sorry, no vacancies. My mum said I was being too idealistic wanting it all straight away. My dad said I should settle for a job with the local newspaper, snapping Miss Gazette opening a shoe shop. No thanks. Now he thinks I'm wasting my degree. I was the first in the family to get one so it's not gone down very well. My head's in the clouds, he said, life's not that easy. But it is for some people, like I said, I see them in here. So why should I be different, have they tried harder or something? Maybe they're lucky or it's because they speak nice. It's so frustrating because I know how good I am. My dad's right, you know, in some ways: I'm stuck here, wasting away. I do it for the money, that's all. But it won't be for ever, no chance. I'm applying for assisting jobs, and as soon as I get one, don't worry, I'm off. I'm now on plan two: Start at the bottom and work up. It might take me years, I know that, but it's what keeps me going between the lager and the leftovers. The fact that I know I'll make it in the end.

The action starts once more. **Carol** *is rather on the outside.* **Mel** *and* **Nicky** *feature.* **Adele** *serves elsewhere.*

Mel   She's funny about that isn't she?

Nicky   Who?

Mel   Carol.

Nicky   Funny about what?

Mel   People thinking she's thick.

Nicky   Well she's only young.

Mel   Yeah, she's a bit of a snob, I mean I don't give a toss what they think about me, but she's always making a point of it. Like she's more special.

Nicky   Well some of us have got ambitions, you know Mel, some of us aren't satisfied with just being here.

Mel   There's nothing wrong with working here. We can't all be brain surgeons Nicky.

Nicky   I know that.

Mel   Oh the way you were talking I thought you were going to tell me you were running off to be chiropodist to the Queen.

Nicky   Not quite.

Carol (*coming to* **Mel** *and* **Nicky**)   Have you seen Mario? He looks like Pavarotti . . . he's strutting about like a prima donna.

Nicky Why? Is he on the war path?

Carol He's got this idea.

Mel What? Is it about the short measures?

Carol I don't believe that man sometimes . . .

Mel What, what, tell us what . . . ?

Nicky Look out, he's watching.

Carol Smile . . .

All Hiya!

*They serve and move away. Contemporary disco music plays. We are in a typical young women's clothing store. The supermarket girls are buying their outfits for the big night. **Mel** has become the shop assistant.*

All Top Shop!

Adele Sharon . . . can't spend a lot . . .

Carol Got a credit card.

Nicky Elaine . . . wanting something special.

Mel Assistant . . . It's three garments and no more.

Carol Where's Susan?

Adele/Nicky Gone to the market . . .

All Uggh!!!!!

Carol Do you have to get really dressed up?

Nicky It's a posh place, yes.

Adele And I'll tell you something, Andy King gets in there!

Nicky Does he?

Adele Yeah I've seen him.

Nicky   Brilliant . . .

Carol   Keep your hands off him you cheeky get, I want him.

Nicky   No chance, I'm the birthday girl!

Mel   How many have you got there love?

Carol   A skirt and some jeans.

Mel   Take this shirt in with you love.

Carol   Yes.

Mel   It's three garments.

Carol   Thanks.

Mel   Just through there . . . three love?

Nicky   Yes.

Mel   In you go.

Adele   I think I've got eleven, I can't decide what to go for.

Mel   Well you'll have to leave some here.

Adele   OK.

Mel   In you go.

Carol
Adele   } Get her . . .
Nicky

Carol   I hate these communal ones, everybody looks at you. (*Looking around.*) I don't like what she's got on.

Adele   I've got one of them.

Carol   Well it's not that bad, just doesn't suit her probably.

Adele   No.

Carol   Have you heard this music, chuffin' hell.

Nicky   Fine Young Cannibals, it's great.

Carol   Not in here though, it feels like Roland Gift's watching you get changed.

Adele   You should be so lucky.

The girls mime undressing. **Mel** (*the assistant*) *watches.*

Carol   Mind you he'd probably be sick if he saw me get changed with my legs.

Adele   There's nothing wrong with your legs.

Carol   There is. They're massive.

Nicky   You're paranoid.

Carol   They are though, look.

Nicky   Don't be daft.

Carol   Mind you when you look at her over there I don't suppose mine are that bad.

Adele   Where?

Carol   In that corner.

Adele   Oh I wouldn't dare.

Nicky   She's no idea.

Adele   Trying a mini skirt on with a figure like that.

Carol   She looks a right state, too thin, she's a stick insect.

Nicky   Look at that one, she's got no bra on.

Adele   Dirty bitch, who does she think she is.

Nicky   Nice tits though.

Adele   Yes.

Carol   Makes my nipples sore that.

Adele   What?

Carol   Not wearing a bra . . .

Nicky   I wish I'd put some decent knickers on.

Carol   I wish I'd shaved my legs . . .

Nicky   She's nice.

Carol   Who?

Nicky   Oh yeah I can see her in the mirror, nice figure.

Carol   Wish I looked like that, the cow.

Adele   She's got a bit of a dog face though.

Carol   Ugly.

Nicky   Yeah.

Adele   I think this is one of them things that look alright on the hanger.

Nicky/Carol   Mmmmmm.

Adele   I'll swop it for something else.

Carol   She's fat, look at her she's fat, she's very fat.

Nicky   Enormous.

Adele   Yes she's fat, she's an elephant.

All   Whew, thank God, someone's fatter than us.

Carol   It's like trying to pack your suitcase when you're going on holiday.

Nicky   What?

Adele   Her trying to get into that. And look at them spots on her back.

Nicky   Horrible.

Carol   I've got spots on my back.

Nicky   But you're not wearing a backless dress.

Carol   We shouldn't say anything, it might be glandular.

Adele   Could be.

Carol   Oh I feel sorry for her don't you?

Nicky   What's this dress look like?

Adele   Oh, it looks lovely that.

Carol   I wish I was as thin as you, you can wear anything.

Nicky   Do you think it's too short?

Adele   No it's lovely.

Carol   Flattering.

Adele   Sexy.

Nicky   I quite like it.

Carol   But it'll look better with stilettos instead of them trainers.

Nicky   I know that stupid. I think I like what she's trying on better.

Carol   No, it looks cheap that, get that, it suits you.

Adele   I don't like any of these. (*To* **Mel**.) Excuse me, excuse me can I swop these for three other things?

Mel   Just come out and get them.

Adele   I can't can I? I'm in my undies. (*To others*.) Silly cow.

Mel   Alright which do you want?

Adele   That blue dress, no the dark one, that skirt and that little top. No, no, that one, that's not mine.

Mel   This one?

Adele   Yes. Thanks, thanks a lot.

Nicky *and* **Carol** *have been trying on clothes.* **Carol** *is struggling into a pair of jeans.*

Carol   I can't get these jeans on me.

Adele   What size are they?

Carol   A ten.

Nicky   They should fit.

Carol   It's my legs, I've told you.

Adele   They're probably small-fitting.

Carol   It's no good, I can't suck my legs in.

Adele   Lie on the floor.

Carol   They're meant for people with no legs.

Adele   You what?

Carol   This style. It's meant for people like you with no legs.

Adele   Skinny legs you mean.

Carol   You know what I mean.

Nicky   Lie down. They'll zip up then, that's what I do with mine.

Carol   I'll feel stupid.

Adele   Lie down.

Nicky   You can't wear jeans tonight anyway.

Carol   I know, but they're for my holidays.

Adele   Bloody hell, Miss Money Bags. Elaine?

Nicky   Alright here we go . . .

Adele   Breathe in!

Carol   I am, you cheeky cow . . .

Nicky   It's no good, it's useless. (**Mel** *is staring at them.*)

Carol   What's she looking at?

Nicky   Take no notice.

Carol   She thinks she's something special just because she works in here.

Adele   Shut up will you and try a bigger size.

Carol   Are you having that dress Elaine?

Nicky   I think so.

Adele   I'm going to get this lycra thing to go with my jacket.

Nicky   Nice. I need some earrings as well.

Carol   Will you wait until I try some more jeans on?

Adele   Well hurry up!

Carol (*leaning out to the assistant with her coat hanger*) Excuse me, could you swop me these for a size twelve?

Mel   I'm sorry but we've no twelves left in that size.

Carol   Have you got any large-fitting tens?

Mel   All our tens are small-fitting.

Carol   Are you sure?

Mel   Absolutely.

Carol   What about a small-fitting fourteen?

Mel   We're all out of fourteens, they've been ever so popular. There should be some more in next week sometime.

Carol   I might call back then.

Mel   Sorry.

Adele   Come on, let's go to C&A.

Music. Back to Shakers.

Nicky Pizza Pepperoni?

Mel One Calzone.

Adele Seafood pasta.

Carol I'm coming through watch your backs please.

Nicky Pizza, Four Seasons.

Mel Pizza Mexicana?

Adele Does anyone want this seafood pasta?

Nicky Pizza Americano?

Mel Mixed salad.

Adele Seafood bleeding pasta anybody?

Carol I'm coming through, one spag bol, with chips.

Nicky Very continental.

Adele Listen, listen stop everything. Somebody in here has ordered seafood pasta, now will you, please, tell me who it is?

Carol (*as a man*) Excuse me!

Adele Is it me or is this place getting worse?

Carol Have you heard about the shorts?

Adele Yeah, but less in the cocktails, what a lousy trick, they're watered down as it is.

Carol No, shorts to wear?

Mel What?

Carol He's got this idea about us wearing shorts.

Mel He's bloody had it, I'm not. What's he want me to wear shorts for? Last week the cheeky bastard said I'd got to lose some weight. I said to him, 'You lose some weight you're nearly as wide as you are tall.'

Adele Why shorts?

Carol   To help boost custom.

Mel   I said to him, 'Hang on I like being this size, Mae West was this size, and nobody complained about her.'

Nicky   Mae West wasn't that big.

Mel   You what?

Nicky   Nothing.

Mel   What did you say?

Nicky   Nothing.

Mel   Mae West was big.

Adele   So when do we have to put 'em on?

Carol   When . . . never.

Adele   Typical.

Carol   What is?

Adele   It's what you expect isn't it, working in a place like this?

Carol   Is it?

Mel   Mind your backs please.

Nicky   Coming through.

Carol   Is it what you expect?

Adele   Table four, oh the fat man's been sick.

All   Oh God . . .

Nicky   Where's the mop?

Adele   It's all over the floor.

Nicky   Oh my it stinks awful.

Mel   What is it?

Adele   I think it's seafood pasta.

Music. Supermarket girls are getting ready for the night ahead.
Nicky *is ironing,* **Carol** *is under a sunlamp,* **Adele** *sits in a face-mask. They are frozen in position until the music finishes.*

All   'Getting ready for the party.'

Adele   Sharon, white-faced.

Carol   Tracey, red-faced and dreaming of sun-kissed beaches.

Nicky   Elaine, dreaming of balloons, party poppers and passionate possibilities.

Mel   Susan, loaded down and late.

All   As usual!

Mel   Hiya everybody, I'm here! Chuffin' buses they're never on time. They make me sick. I've bought my heated bendy rollers and my tongs and my diffuser so my hair doesn't go frizzy. I've got some gel and wax and thickening lotion but I couldn't find my mousse so you'll have to lend me some.

Nicky   You won't be able to hold your head up if you put all that stuff on. Hiya Susan.

Mel   Hi. (*To audience.*) She gets right up my arse, her.

Nicky (*to audience*)   She gets right on my tits.

Mel   Anyway, I've got some of them More cigarettes as well, long and brown I think they look great.

Nicky   Don't smoke them near me, I can't stand it, it'll make my dress stink.

Mel   Don't worry I won't. What's up with Shaz? Aren't you talking or what?

Adele (*through an almost closed mouth as if wearing a face-mask*)   I can't.

Mel   You what?

Nicky   She can't.

Mel   Uggh! What's that stuff on your face?

Adele   Face-mask.

Mel (*picking up an imaginary bottle and reading*)   'Avocado and cucumber, the first step to a more beautiful you.' I'll tell you something, it's definitely working. You look a lot better with that on than you ever did before.

Adele   Don't make me laugh.

Nicky   Don't make her laugh.

Mel   Aggh, don't move it's cracking.

Adele   Go away, go away will you!

Mel   Too late, it's gone.

Adele   Shit.

Mel   You'll be alright . . .

Adele   Well I have had it on ages. (*She mimes removing the face-mask and makes appropriate noises.*)

Nicky   I've finished with the ironing-board Shaz.

Carol (*coming out of freeze*)   What am I gonna do? Look at my face!

Nicky   It's bright red.

Carol   I know that.

Mel   What's happened?

Adele   She's been on the sunbed.

All   Oooo . . . errr.

Carol   I've only had fifty minutes.

Adele   You're not used to it.

Mel   It's because you've got fair skin.

Carol   I can't go out like this.

Nicky   Powder it down.

Carol   I can try.

Adele   I'm going to have a bath. (*She uses the bar as a bath.*)

Mel   Shit. There's a ladder in my tights.

Carol   I've got to shave my armpits yet.

Mel   And I only bought them today.

Nicky   I've got some spare ones in my bag.

Mel   They won't fit me.

Adele   They will, they fit any size. (*Grimace to audience from girls.*)

Carol   Have you got any hair-removing cream?

Adele   In the bathroom!

Carol   Thanks.

Nicky   I'll have to cover up my spot.

Carol   I'll have to cover up my face.

Mel   Can I borrow some perfume, I love that Giorgio.

Adele   Plug in them rollers, I'll need them in a minute.

Nicky   They won't work if your hair's wet.

Adele   I'm going to dry it first.

Carol   Will you put my nail varnish on for me, I can't do it with my left hand.

Nicky   No, go away you stink of hair remover.

Carol (*as if it's on her legs and under her armpits*)   I've got to give it ten minutes.

Nicky Phewgh, you're like a dog that's been out in the rain. Can I borrow your mascara?

Mel Yes . . . Do I look fat in this dress?

All (*unconvincingly*) No . . .

Adele You look alright.

Mel But does my bum look massive?

Adele Your hair looks really nice.

Carol I look like a tomato and smell like an old dishcloth.

Nicky Do you think Andy King will turn up?

All God, Andy King!

Mel Why?

Nicky Just wondered.

Carol Oh yes?

Nicky Our Sandra said he told her he thought I was alright.

Adele He never!

Nicky He did.

Carol He's gorgeous, he can put his slippers under my bed any time.

Mel Tracey! God!

Adele Well you've got no chance 'cos it sounds like it's Elaine he's after.

Carol Well that's bloody typical that is. Listen can you see my blackheads?

Nicky I hope he will be there, you never know what might happen.

Adele Can you see my double chin?

Mel   Can you smell my hair spray?

Carol   Can you smell my bad breath?

Nicky   Can you see my VPL?

All   Oh we'll never be ready!

Music. Back at the bar. The girls as waitresses again.

Nicky   Have you seen what some of these girls are wearing? Fashion victims.

Carol   Thank you Selina Scott.

Adele   Is it OK, but I'll have to go early?

Mel   You what?

Adele   I'll have to go early.

Mel   What for?

Adele   Get the last bus.

Mel   What's up with taxis?

Adele   Are you going to pay for one?

Mel   No.

Adele   Well I'll have to go half an hour early then.

Mel   Oh right, I'll go early as well then.

Adele   Don't be childish.

Mel   I want to get home and see Steve, I don't want to be here, I can think of better things to do.

Adele   It's only this once.

Mel   I've heard that before.

Carol   What's your problem Mel? You're getting engaged, you're doing what you want.

Mel   Well look this is a job, we get paid to work so many hours, let's work them. I'll tell you what Adele.

Why don't you just come in on Thursdays?

Nicky   What, every Thursday?

Adele   I'm not talking to you, you're not worth it Melanie.

Nicky   Oh Melanie . . . ?

Carol   I'll cover Adele's tables.

Mel   That's not the point is it? We're always covering for you in some way, I'm pig sick of covering for her.

Adele   Alright you go early all next week, I'll make arrangements, I'll cover for you.

Carol   What is the point Mel, I don't get it?

Mel   The point is, she should either have a job or be a mother.

Adele   Millions do both.

Mel   Do they?

Adele   They have to.

Mel   You can't do both it's obvious.

Adele   And you know do you?

Mel   I know we're carrying you.

Adele   How am I supposed to live? I don't even get maintenance payments.

Mel   And you're never here on time. What is it between you and Mario eh? It can't be doing a three-year-old much good being dragged around to God knows where every night. Then being collected by her mother in the morning.

Adele   That's why I want to go early.

Mel   I mean the poor kid won't know where she is.

Adele   Don't you bring Emma into this, because you

don't know shit from butter.

Mel Don't I?

Nicky Never eat her sandwiches Adele.

Mel You think you know everything don't you?

Nicky Hey come on you two, leave it. There's a lot to do without all this.

Adele Shut up Nicky.

Nicky Don't start on me.

Adele Just keep your beak out.

Nicky Oh I like how it's all suddenly my fault.

Adele Just shut up.

Nicky Sorry I spoke.

Carol Let's forget it, people are looking.

Adele Let them.

Carol Adele? Don't . . .

Adele Let 'em, let 'em look. I'm not bothered. Let the whole lot of 'em look, I couldn't give a toss.

Mel She'll end up like her mother, if you ask me.

Carol Let it drop now.

Mel And let's face it, her mother doesn't know where she is . . .

Nicky Leave it Melanie . . .

Mel Doesn't know what she wants.

Adele Why? Do you?

Carol Hey come on leave it alone, everybody's looking over here.

Mel I know what I want . . .

Adele   Do you?

Mel   Yeah I do. And I wouldn't treat a kid of mine like that.

Adele   Wouldn't you?

Nicky   Let's just get on with the job shall we?

Mel   No I wouldn't ... I mean look at yourself Adele, your life's an accident just waiting to happen.

Adele   Let me tell you something, my little girl wants for nothing, she's happy, and she loves me and I love her more than you'll ever love anybody. Because you're too bitter and twisted to love anybody except yourself.

Mel   Piss off!

Adele   I hope Steve realises what he's letting himself in for.

Mel   Well he won't run off with somebody else, I'll tell you that much.

Adele   And you're sure of that are you?

Mel   Yeah I am.

Adele   Yeah I thought that I was sure. I thought it was going to be all hearts and flowers. Me and Craig were the perfect couple. Holding hands and kissing in public. Love's sweet dream ... then Emma came along.

Carol   Leave it Adele.

Mel   Well you know what you could have done.

Adele   He wanted me to, she was an accident, anyway obviously I didn't. Debts built up, we started to argue, he started staying out, sounds like the routine thing but when it happens to you you can't believe it.

Nicky   Did you know her?

Adele   I'd seen her. What hurt the most was that he told me he was looking for work. But he wasn't he was looking for her, and then he'd come home and I'd cook him his teas. So when you're cooking Steve's tea don't ask him where he's been, because if he's lying, it'll tear you up inside.

Mel   Yeah thanks I'll bear that in mind.

Adele   I want to get out, I do, I want to get out of this rut, break away. I can't stand the facade, the show, the smiling, the grinning, the sniggers behind your back, the comments, the insulting tips, the pretence that what we're offering is a touch of class. I need something more than this, I need something that I can grab a hold of, something that I can call mine. I don't need a man, don't get me wrong, I thought I did, I don't, what I want is another chance. A chance to start over . . . And you know I probably would wear the shorts if he asks us, I'd probably go topless, get my tits out, wear tassels on the ends, and paint them the colours of the rainbow. I'd probably do whatever it needs to stay here, because at the moment, I've got no choice. I can't see anything that's going to make things better for me. Right now wearing a pair of shorts in a bar is just a matter of acceptance, because there's nothing else. It's just a teardrop in an ocean of worries.

All   Can we have some service.

Adele   Coming . . .

The birthday girls enter Shakers all excited. They have already had a few drinks.

Carol   What about this? ZZZZZZZZ.

Adele   You daft cow, look at me, I'm covered in silly string!

Mel   You look like a shopping basket.

Nicky   We've got a table booked.

Carol   It's her birthday!

Mel   Isn't it fantastic!

Nicky   I think we're sitting over there.

Adele   I love the colours.

Mel   I love the tables.

Carol   I love it all, it's gorgeous.

Nicky   Is Andy King here?

Carol   Can't see him. Ooo, that wine's made me giggly has it you? (*All giggle.*)

Adele   We're going to have a great time.

Mel   We're going to have a laugh.

Nicky   Is Andy King here?

Adele   I'm having a prawn cocktail, garlic bread, spaghetti bolognese, a side salad, chocolate ice cream and a coffee.

Carol   Listen to her, you've not even looked at the menu.

Adele   It's what I always have.

Nicky   Shall we have a drink first?

Mel   Another!

All   Yeah!

Carol   Let's all have a Bloody Mary.

Adele   Bloody hell!

Nicky   Four Bloody Marys!

Mel   I love birthdays!

Carol   I do.

Mel   Bloody hell it's strong.

Carol   What is?

Mel   Bloody Mary.

Adele   Oh I love it in here, it's fantastic.

Nicky   Oh my God.

Adele   It's so classy.

Mel   I know it's brilliant.

Nicky   Oh God . . . look . . .

Carol   What?

Nicky   Look there.

Adele   Where?

Nicky   There, there, don't all look at once.

Mel   Where?

Nicky   Oh God. Look who it is.

Carol   Which one?

Mel   Who do you mean, pizza-face?

Adele   Ughhh.

Nicky   No no . . . oh I can't move . . . look.

Mel   Where where . . . ?

Adele   Who is it?

Carol   What's she on about?

Nicky   Oh God I just can't believe it . . . it's him!

All   Who? (*A beat.*)

Nicky   Andy King!

Music. The four girls react as if they have seen Andy King, and they blow kisses and wave to him and the lights fade to black.

Act Two

The set as before. House lights, music. The four actresses are on stage, in a freeze. Lights, and with energy they come downstage as the 'boys'.

Carol And in we come, straight out of the car, straight into the bar.

Adele The boys is what we are.

Mel Dressed in our designer gear.

Nicky Looking like men who drink Belgian beer.

Mel We are talced and fresh, wearing splash-on Polo, and minty foot deodorant.

Carol And teeth gleaming white, like George Michael.

Nicky It's cold outside but we don't care, a flimsy top is all we wear.

Adele We arrive at the door, our hair gel in place, and our car keys dangling from our fingertips.

Nicky Hi.

Carol Hi.

Mel Hi.

Carol We assume that everyone in the bar is watching our every step.

Mel Our every move.

Carol (*hands through hair*) I am gorgeous.

Adele So am I.

Nicky I love myself.

Carol We coolly adjust ourselves. (*They adjust their crotch.*) And laugh nervously. (*All nervously laugh.*)

Nicky We look cool but sexy. Like a cross between Tom Cruise and River Phoenix.

Adele A sort of river cruise.

Mel And the gum? (*They all mime the gum.*)

Nicky In goes the gum.

All Thud. (*As the gum enters their mouth.*) Chew. (*They chew the gum.*)

Adele And another casual look around the place, eye out for the skirt.

Mel If it moves take it to bed, if not stick it on your windscreen. Mark and Bernice, Radio One FM, the business.

Nicky Trev and Val Radio One road show.

Carol Sound your horn if you had sex last night.

All (*horn*) Road hog.

Nicky And surfers do it stood up. (*Laugh.*)

Carol Rugby players do it in the scrum. (*Laugh.*)

Mel Sky divers do it head first. (*Laugh.*)

Adele Hairdressers do it from behind.

All Wooooooooohhh.

Adele And then I spot one. Oh yes, behind a plastic palm, sat near Andy King.

Mel Andy King? Is he in?

Carol Over there?

Nicky A God amongst men.

Mel Who is he with . . . ?

Carol He looks fantastic.

All Yeah.

Adele Oh look, the bird sat near Andy King, she's walking to the cig machine. Big tits, no tights, arse like a peach. I'd like to bite into that.

Carol Where is she?

Adele Passing one of the waitresses.

Carol Oh yeah.

Adele Over my left shoulder, two o'clock to the bar, five o'clock to the ciggy machine. (**Mel** *has become the girl.*)

Carol Nice one.

Adele So over to the ciggy machine I glide. (**Adele** *crosses to* **Mel** *who is at a cigarette machine.*)

Mel Shit.

Adele Isn't it working?

Mel No. (*To audience.*) He thinks that I'm a bimbo but I'm really intelligent.

Adele Let me have a quick look. Huhu. A masculine boot should sort this out. I do Thai kick-boxing you see. There, boot. (*Mimes a boot.*) There we are. Look doll, twenty John Player Specials.

Mel Thanks.

Adele No problem. My name's Matt.

Mel Thanks Matt, but I wanted Benson & Hedges, bye.

Adele She walks off, shit, lost my cool.

Nicky What happened?

Adele Oh man.

Mel (*now one of the boys again*) Go on what happened?

Adele What a dog, breath like camel shit.

Mel   She looks fantastic.

Adele   Yeah but up close, really rough, I think, she's married, she's deaf, she's blind she's fat, she's broke my cool, let's laugh it off.

Carol   What happened, what went wrong?

Adele   I just can't understand it.

Mel   Did you tell her you wear Ted Baker shirts?

Adele   I said I know the Blow Monkeys, watch MTV and shop at Paul Smith.

Mel   Did you shave?

Adele   With Ronson.

Nicky   What about teeth?

Adele   Plax mouthwash.

Nicky   Armpits.

Adele   Armani roll-on.

Mel   Maybe she thought you were dull?

Adele   Give us a break.

Nicky   Maybe she thought you were gay?

Adele   Come on?

Carol   Maybe she just wasn't interested . . .

All   Don't talk crap!

Adele   Let's have another round of Malibu and piss off down to Browns. Yeah.

All   Yeah.

Adele   Great stuff.

All   Hey you. I'll have a Marra Bubu.

Carol   What's a Marra Bubu?

All   Nothing Yogi.

Nicky   Let's get some more drinks.

All   Yeah.

Carol   Hey you, can we have some service?

Mel   Come on love.

Adele   Can we have some service down the cool end of the bar darlin'?

Mel   Hey you with the tits, what you doing later? Well do it on your own you ugly cow!

Adele   She really is ugly. Hey call the ugly police.

Carol   Can we have some service?

Adele   Hey you. At last. What do we want?

Nicky   I'll have a Malibu.

Mel   And me.

Carol   And me.

All   Right, another round of Malibus.

The boys dissolve to waitresses.

Mel   Another round of farts.

Adele   Posey bastards.

Carol   I bet they're loaded that lot, got their money from Daddy's business. I've seen tramps with more manners.

Nicky   They're just having a night out, having a laugh.

Mel   At whose expense?

Adele   You're lively at this hour aren't you?

Mel   I think she's on a promise.

Carol   Yeah it's the bloke with the big ears and the glasses.

Mel   What, Pebble-dash Man?

Nicky (*joking*)   Chance would be a fine thing.

Adele   Maybe it's the Wig Man but she daren't tell us?

Nicky   Like I said, I've had some good news today, that's all.

Mel   What?

Nicky (*to* **Mel**)   Look at you.

Adele   Go on, what is it?

Nicky   Ah ha, interested are you?

Carol   Anything to get out of here.

Nicky   Yeah well I've got a job.

Mel   Oh yeah what doing, dressing up in a bear's outfit and handing out leaflets?

Nicky   No, but it's something different.

Mel   So is dressing up as a bear.

Nicky   Dancing.

Adele   Where?

Nicky   On a cruise.

Mel   A cruise.

Carol   How long have you been dancing?

Nicky   I've done it for years, from being a kid.

Adele   When do you start?

Nicky   In a month.

The others are green with envy.

Carol   A month, that's good that's great, well done. That's great. A cruise?

Mel   My sister went on a cruise. It's a bit boring . . . She didn't like it.

Adele   You'll see the world.

Carol   I think it's great.

Adele   Where do you go first?

Carol   Bahamas would be nice.

Adele   Or Florida.

Nicky   Norway.

Mel   Eh? You'll freeze to death.

Carol   Norway.

Mel   What's in Norway?

Carol   Fjords. Snow. Saunas.

Adele   Norway?

Carol   Pine furniture.

Nicky   Think of me in a month's time, the lights, the roar of the greasepaint, the smell of the crowd. I've always wanted to do it and at last I'm giving it a go.

Mel   I don't fancy that, living out of a suitcase. I wouldn't like it, I like my home comforts too much.

Carol   Cross-country skiing . . .

Mel   I'm happy being normal.

Nicky   You're normal?

Carol   You'll send us a postcard won't you Nicky?

Nicky   Course I will.

Adele   A cruise you lucky sod.

Mel   Yeah but Norway?

Carol   Could be worse.

Mel   Could it?

*The lights fade. A spotlight outlines **Nicky**. The others freeze.*

Nicky   I know they're jealous of me. I don't blame
them, no one wants to stay here. It's funny though
now I can escape, I'm bloody scared to death. Nine
months, it's a long time, what if I don't make any
friends? What if I get seasick, or food poisoning, or get
lost somewhere in a forest and have to live with a tribe
of eskimos and never come home again? I know I'm
being stupid. My mind's gone haywire. But deep down
I'm a panicker, I can't help it, but I am. And I know
it's what I want, but in reality it's frightening leaving it
all . . . your mum, your dad, your mates. I'm excited
as well though, don't get me wrong. I wouldn't forego
the opportunity, it's a chance in a lifetime: travel,
freedom, celebrity. Oh yeah, I've definitely got to go!
But the actual job? I wouldn't tell the others but more
than anything I'm apprehensive about that. I've got to
lose some weight for a start, some of the costumes are
ever so small, sequins and all that stuff, but there is
some topless as well. It's classy, it's all part of the
dancing. But it's getting over that first time isn't it?
Then I'm sure I'll be alright. You see to be honest it
took me about four days to get them out when we
went to Ibiza and then I laid on my front. I suppose
though they're alright, even though I'm not Bridget
Nielson. And they did look at them so if they were
awful they wouldn't have had me. Like I said I'm sure
I'll get used to it. It's all the excitement, it makes you
nervous I don't know black from white. But I'm sure it
will be brilliant, I'm sure it will. I mean the world will
be my oyster, I can't believe it! That's the thing
though isn't it? What do you do when a dream comes
true? What do you dream of then?

Carol *and* **Mel** *are seated at two chairs. They are Mr and Mrs Trendy.* **Nicky** *watches as* **Adele** *takes the order.*

Adele   One tired waitress.

Nicky   One Tom Collins.

Carol   One trendy couple. In deep fried love.

Mel   Oh look at the menu. It's shaped like a cocktail shaker, isn't that clever. It's been designed that way.

Carol (*trendy man*)   Yes that's why it's called Shakers.

They laugh.

Mel   That's right. What do you fancy darling?

Carol   What I fancy isn't on the menu.

Mel   Oh you're awful.

Carol   I know.

Adele   Excuse me, are we ready to order?

Carol (*abrupt*)   We haven't had time to look at the menu yet.

Adele   Sorry sir. I'll pop back in a moment. (*Aside.*) Twat.

Mel   I'd like to lick you all over.

Carol   I don't know where to start. (*The menu.*)

Mel   Did you hear me?

Carol   You're wicked.

Adele   I think I've pulled a bad straw.

Nicky   They look like a nice couple.

Adele   Nice. Very nice. Jesus, these shoes.

Mel   Excuse me. (*Attracting attention.*) Excuse me . . . oi oi.

Carol   Hello, hello.

Nicky   I think they want to order.

Carol   Hello.

Adele   I'm on my way. (**Adele** *crosses.*) Ready to order, sir?

Carol   Yes we'd like to start with garlic sweetcorn.

Adele   Of course.

Mel   Oh no, I want the paté, I must have the paté.

Carol   Do you have any paté?

Adele   Sir?

Mel   What sort of paté do you have?

Adele   What sort do you want you silly-looking gett!

Mel   I'm awfully sorry?

Adele   Madam, duck paté, liver paté.

Mel   I'll have the duck paté.

Carol   One garlic sweetcorn, one duck paté, I'll take the lasagna, and Clarissa?

Mel   Could I, um. Have the . . .

Adele   Come on pig-breath.

Mel   Oh erm. Steak au poivre . . . no no.

Adele   Hurry up.

Mel   Is the beef British?

Adele   Madam.

Mel   Oh right, I'll try the . . . oh no, I'll have the . . . erm, pasta, no no . . . I'll take the . . .

Adele   For fuck's sake!

Mel   I'll have the fillet.

Adele Certainly madam. French fries, pomme frites? Side salad, baked potato?

Mel Sorry.

Adele Are you flaming deaf, chips, lettuce or jacket spud?

Mel I'll take the green salad, must watch the figure.

Adele Certainly. Wine?

Mel Oh wine, wine.

Carol Wine?

Mel Oh yes darling, wine, wine.

Carol Do you have any wine?

Adele It's on the back of the bloody menu.

Carol (*turns over menu*) Ah, ah here it is. Been there all the time. I think we'll take the Châteauneuf du Pape.

Adele Certainly. Would you like two straws?

Carol Sorry.

Adele I'll bring it straight away sir.

Nicky And yet on the other hand there is always the couple who are not *au courant*.

Mel *and* **Carol** *become Mr and Mrs Very Untrendy.*

Mel Menu's good in't it?

Carol What's it supposed to be?

Mel Pepperpot isn't it?

Carol I thought it was a flask. What do you fancy?

Mel Don't know.

Carol I fancy a lot of something, I'm starved.

Adele Excuse me sir, ready to order?

Carol No.

Adele Oh right, I'll be over by the bar, if you need me.

Carol I'll give you a shout.

Mel I don't know where to start.

Carol What's this 'Entrees'?

Mel Dunno . . .

Carol Oi, oi. (**Adele** *goes to them.*)

Adele Ready to order sir?

Carol Yes. I want the garlic sweetcorn. And two pints of lager and a bottle of red plonk.

Adele Of course.

Carol And she'll have the payt . . .

Adele Payt?

Carol Yeah a big slice of liver payt.

Mel And I want more than three slices of toast.

Adele See what I can do.

Mel And a lot of butter, not just one frozen notch.

Adele Certainly.

Carol And two lasag-nees.

Adele Would you like some chips and red sauce sir?

Nicky One Zombie Voodoo. A Harvey Wallbanger. And one Screwdriver coming up.

Adele One Mary Stewart. And a Johnny From London.

Mel (*as* **Mel**, *moving*) Things are very hot.

Carol (*as* **Carol**, *moving*)   Getting pretty hectic.

Adele   Behind the bar and in the kitchen.

Nicky   Palms are sweating, feet are itching.

Adele   Every order is taken with a smile.

All   Cheers.

Nicky   Every bad joke returned with panache.

All   Oh that's really funny. (*A beat.*) Yawn.

Adele   Ten o'clock and the place is heaving.

Nicky   The only room is on the ceiling. One Blue
Bols, one Sidecar.

Carol   Banana Monster.

Through this last order **Nicky** *and* **Carol** *have become a
couple. They are seated.* **Mel** *and* **Adele** *make cocktails.*

Adele   Oh God I think I've got this wrong now.

Mel   You what?

Adele   I messed this up. I've got a Havana Zombie
mixed up with a Salty Dog.

Mel   Well what are you making, a Dog Zombie?

Adele   It's supposed to be a Gin Sling.

Mel   Could be a Salty Zombie.

Adele   Help me Mel. I've wasted loads of booze, I've
got all the names mixed up in my head.

Mel   It's because your mind's not on the job.

Adele   What am I going to do?

Mel   Who is it for?

Adele   The posh couple.

Nicky   You Uuuuu . . .

Adele Oh God they've seen me.

Mel Just give it to her, it's a nice colour.

Adele It doesn't look much like a Gin Sling though does it?

Mel Say it's a special.

Adele A special what?

Mel I don't know, you're supposed to be the expert.

Adele *takes the cocktail to the waiting couple.*

Carol At last.

Adele Yes sorry about the wait, here's your cocktail . . .

Carol I ordered a Gin Sling.

Adele I know.

Carol Fine, take that away.

Adele Well you see you are our hundredth customer tonight, and so you win the surprise cocktail.

Carol But we've only just arrived and the place is seething.

Adele Hundredth cocktail customer, I mean.

Carol Oh well.

Nicky That's great, thank you.

Adele Yes so you win tonight's surprise cocktail.

Nicky Wonderful.

Carol What's in it?

Adele That's the surprise.

Carol It tastes yummy. What's it called?

Adele It's erm. (*She looks around for inspiration.*) Oh erm

. . . Emergency Exit.

Carol   Oh, potent is it?

Adele   You bet.

Nicky   Do you know I'm sure they make up these ridiculous names on the spur of the moment. You couldn't make me the Two Hind Legs Of An African Elephant could you?

The couple laugh.

Carol   Oh, Gerald.

Adele   Don't be so smart, you silly-looking bastard.

Nicky   Sorry?

Adele   I'm sorry sir, I'm afraid I don't know that one.

Nicky   It was a joke.

Nicky *laughs. Suddenly the four waitresses remember something. They have forgotten to sing to the birthday party. They rush around the stage, find the area where the birthday party group are sat.*

All   Oh no . . .

They regroup. The four waitresses stand in a line and sing 'Happy Birthday' to four imaginary girls who are seated in a semi-circle in front of them. This is a routine which the cocktail waitresses are familiar with, however, on this occasion, they have omitted to discover the name of the person whose birthday it is, all saying different names together. Finally, they take four stools and become the girls at the party.

Adele   It's getting late . . .

Mel   The restaurant's full . . .

Carol   But in their little space . . .

Nicky   The birthday girl is tipsy and glowing in her lace . . .

Mel She's had three more Bloody Marys.

Adele . . . And so have Sharon . . .

Mel Sue . . .

Carol And Trace . . .

All hiccup.

Mel That dress is smashing, I love it, I do I love it. Where did you get it? French Connection?

Carol No, got it at George.

Mel George?

Carol Yeah, George at Asda.

Mel Oh it's lovely that.

Carol It's nice here innit?

Nicky Haven't you been before?

Adele We used to come every Thursday after aerobics.

Nicky We think we saw Jonathan Ross in here once, he was on location. He's ever so tall.

Carol I don't like him.

Nicky I don't.

Mel Does he play the piano with that group?

Adele No, that's Jools Holland. Jonathan Ross is the one with the suits.

Mel Oh him, he's got a beard, does *The Clothes Show*.

Carol That's Jeff Banks. Somebody switch her off.

Nicky It's packed out tonight.

Adele It's warm.

Nicky   I'm spinning.

Carol   My face is on fire.

Mel   Don't worry you look alright.

Nicky   If you like tomatoes.

All laugh. **Adele** *becomes the waitress.*

Adele   And then: a flash, a scintilla! For Elaine a birthday treat. A crushed ice candy cocktail with a sparkler in it.

Mel   Mind your hair, it'll set on fire!

Carol   Isn't it brilliant.

Adele   Very, very neat.

All   Oh isn't it nice. Lovely. It's great!

Nicky   Oh no, everyone's looking.

Adele   They're all glad it's not them.

Nicky   I'm embarrassed, God I'm embarrassed. Can you see Andy King?

Carol   Can I hell, it's choc-a-bloc.

Mel   Isn't that him over there?

Nicky   Where? Oh yeah, he's looking at us, he can see me!

Carol   I feel tiddly, I think it's this drink.

Adele (*who has now become Sharon*)   He's waving.

Nicky   He's not! Can he see it's my birthday?

Mel   I think so, they're all waving. Come on wave at them. (**Mel** *begins to wave.*) Hey up. Ooooh.

Nicky   Don't!

Carol   It's her birthday.

Nicky   Oh no!

Adele   Twenty-one you cheeky sods.

Mel   I think he winked at you.

Nicky   Oh my heart's going, I've come over all queer.

Carol   He's with somebody, she's just come back from the toilet!

Mel   Oh yes.

Nicky   Oh God.

Adele   She's attractive.

Nicky   Oh well. I don't suppose he's that nice anyway . . .

Carol   Hey watch this. A party popper!

The miming of the party popper presents fun as we see it explode in the air.

Adele   I've had a monster Piña Colada, I feel great!

Mel   I feel a bit sick, it's this wine. I'm not used to it.

Nicky   Do you think he's been going out with her long?

Adele   Hey! Crackers . . .

All   Ohhh! Yeahhhh! (*They mime the pulling of crackers, put on the hats, etc.*)

Mel   I've got a ring.

All   Urrerrmmm.

Adele   I've got a hat. It's daft.

Nicky   It suits you.

Carol   Hey listen to this. 'The more you take the more you leave behind.' What is it?

Adele   Tablets?

Mel   Water?

Nicky   Girlfriends.

Mel   What?

Carol   Steps, the more steps.

All   Oh yeah, good that.

Carol   A toast to Elaine, twenty-one today.

Adele   God bless you love.

They all sing a verse of 'Twenty-One Today'.

Nicky (*sings*)   Happy birthday to you . . .

Nicky *is away, she improvises a tune, freezes upstage.* **Carol**, **Adele** *and* **Mel** *are downstage.*

Mel   Nicky is unbelievable. She is always over the top. I mean who does she think she is, Bonnie Langford?

Adele   She's happy that's all.

Mel   Do you really think she'll make it?

Carol   Don't know. If she's determined.

Mel   I don't think she will.

Adele   So that's the kiss of death for her . . . ?

Carol   Why not?

Mel   I don't know. I think it's her nose. Her face, something. I wouldn't go on a cruise no way. It's something . . .

Carol   Like what?

Mel   She's really too short for a dancer. That's why she's going on a cruise. If she was tall she'd be going to be a bluebell girl. You see I know about these

things. My cousin was an understudy on *Cats*, she was
six foot two.

Carol Oh right.

Mel In nine months' time she'll be coming back here
with her tail between her legs, asking Mario for work.

Carol I wouldn't argue about it. This place is going
to close.

Mel You what?

Carol It's going to change hands anyway.

Mel You know what it'll be, a few new palms, a coat
of paint, maybe some foreign beers, and it's more or
less the same. We'll still be here. It's happening all
over, it's like spring cleaning.

Carol So the punters think they're getting something
new.

Mel Maybe it'll become a MacDonald's.

Carol God forbid.

Mel Well there isn't a MacDonald's around here for
nearly two hundred yards.

Carol Do you know what is in a Big Mac?

Adele Don't please.

Mel It could be like one of those trendy new places,
there's one in Covent Garden. Thank God it's Sunday.

Carol Fridays.

Mel You speak for yourself Carol.

Adele Oh we are on the ball tonight.

Mel It'll be one of those places where the waitresses
are employed because they are witty and smart.

Carol Unless here, where they're shitty and fart . . . ?

Adele   Does that include you?

Mel   You know the sort of place I'm on about, they wear odd socks and bumpers and wear hats with dog turds on them.

Adele   Very witty.

Carol   Very smart.

Mel   Joke turds. You can wear what you want, as long as it's stupid.

Carol   Sounds like hell.

Mel   And they play jazz music, and have trombones that come through the ceiling and pianos that play by themselves.

Carol   It is hell.

Mel   Oh I think that'd be good. You could wear something different every day. I'd wear a badge on my bust with very small writing on it. It would say 'If you can read this, you are two foot too close so knob off . . .'

Adele   Well I wish you luck.

Carol   Secretly, you really like it here don't you? Even though you complain all the time?

Mel   It's like this Carol, in the mad bad world as long as you do your job, you can complain as much as you want. No one can sack you for complaining, they can only get rid of you if you don't work.

Carol   That sounds subversive.

Mel   Common sense if you ask me, take the money, complain as much as you want, and then run. Or in my case hobble.

Adele   Sounds to me like you've got it all worked out.

Mel   Yeah it does doesn't it?

Adele   Yeah.

Mel   Yeah that's me kid.

Adele   Everything in its place and a place for everything!

Mel   Yeah lucky old Mel.

Adele   You'll probably be here when you're sixty.

Mel   If I'm lucky.

Adele   Full of ambition aren't you?

Mel   Actually I am, yeah.

Adele   Day in day out, no change. 'Mel the constant'. You should put that on a badge and all.

Mel   Yeah I might do.

Adele   No troubles and no bloody worries . . .

The lights slowly fade. **Mel** *steps forward.*

Mel   This job's not bad you know. I used to work in the supermarket, now that was mindless, sat about all day, bored out of your head, dreaming of the weekend. At least when you're here you can have the odd cig and a natter. You see I just want an easy life, no pressures. And I want someone to care for me, and I think I've found that with Steve, I do. Adele thinks she's the only one with problems. Oh God who is she kidding? Talk about skeletons in the cupboard, I've got a kitchen suite full of them. You see there's something I've got to tell Steve; I think it's only fair. You see when I was sixteen I used to go to this tacky bar with my mates. I thought it was neat. It had an awful painting of the Manhattan skyline right around the walls. And a drawing of the Statue of Liberty that was about nine times too big sticking up from behind a skyscraper. The New York Bar . . . oh what? . . . I

thought it was great. And I met this bloke there. Pete,
he was a barman. He was a lot older than me and
really good-looking. I thought he was great. We had a
brilliant time, a lot of laughs and I was still a virgin.
He didn't force me to sleep with him, but I fancied
him that much and it seemed the most exciting thing
ever, that I couldn't help myself. I wasn't stupid
though. I tried to get on the pill but I'd had jaundice
when I was a kid, so I ended up with a cap. I'm not
kidding, they're a right pain in the neck. I've got a coil
now so it's OK. Anyway we went on holiday for two
weeks to Scotland, I told my mum that I was going
with my mates. I thought I was pregnant when I went
but I didn't tell anyone. I was frightened, so I put it to
the back of my mind. But it was impossible because I
kept seeing pregnant women and mothers with
pushchairs and tiny clothes on hangers and babies in
magazines. So I went into the chemist and searched
amongst the Durex for a DIY testing kit. Back in the
camp site toilets I weed all over my hands trying to get
it in the test tube. Why do they make them so small?
Two hours later the change in colour and the sickness
in my stomach said everything. I didn't really have
time to think about it. I asked for an abortion. I mean
neither me or Pete wanted to have this thing that
would tie us down for ever ... It's a big responsibility.
And what would my mum have said or my mates on
the YTS? And what about the rest of our lives? I was
scared as well, how could I look after a kid? I only
had two GCSEs. I begged them to let me have it done
up there in Scotland, so no one would know. They put
me in this hospital by the sea. There were about eight
of us in the ward. All the others had fluffy slippers and
dressing gowns and orange juice by their beds. I had
to make do with a hospital nightie, my stocking feet
and a baggy combat jumper I'd taken camping with
me. It's soon done, you bleed a lot and feel depressed,
but it is a relief as well. Sometimes I think about it,

what it would be like now. It upset me. I want to tell
people, talk about it, but I can't. The thing is should I
tell Steve? We want to get married and I know this
time it's right. He's got a good job, he's a roadie with
a rock band, we might even be able to buy a house. I
want to tell him because I want to be honest. But it
can stop you having kids altogether can't it? I'm
frightened that if he knows he'll leave me. No, I think
I'll keep it a secret between me and you. Don't tell
anyone, will you?

*The lights fade slowly. Slow music. The evening is creeping by.
Lights fade at the end of* **Mel***'s speech. A sudden rush of energy,
as a theatre crowd returns to Shakers for a post-show drink.*

Carol   Darling?

Mel   Darling?

Carol   Darling's over here by the window.

Adele   What a wonderful show.

Nicky   Wonderful.

Mel   I thought she was amazing.

Carol   Wasn't she just.

Adele   Breathtaking. I've seen all his work. Donald
and I listen to the show on CD.

Mel   It really is the only way to listen.

Carol   I wish I'd seen Elaine Page.

Mel   We saw her in London, she was ever so good.
And do you know she's only quite tiny.

Adele   Excuse me waitress, we're ready to order.

Nicky   It's based on a true story, apparently there
was an Eva Peron.

Carol   Really?

Nicky   Oh yes and she was Argentinian.

Carol   Isn't that amazing?

Adele   I thought it was a touch too long.

Mel   Yes I'd trim the second act.

Adele   But I wouldn't cut the interval. Waitress?

Mel   Oh no I thought the interval was marvellous.

Carol   Anyone for a drink?

All   I'll say. Yes. I think we all are.

Mel   Terry saw him at the health club.

Adele   Who?

Mel   Che Guevara.

All   Really.

Carol   Sidonie has bought a new horse, did I tell you?

All   Really?

Mel   Have you heard about the new F-Plan diet. Apparently you can lose fifteen stone in a day.

All   Really?

Nicky   Well I was talking to one of the gals at the club and she said there was still a National Health Service.

All   Really?

Adele   Where?

Nicky   I think she said somewhere in Scotland.

Mel   Oh yes I think I've heard of Scotland.

Adele   Don't you think it's marvellous now we all live in a classless society?

All   Oh yes.

Mel   Oh yes.

Carol   Oh look at the chef.

During this **Mel** *has become the chef.*

Adele/Nicky   Oh isn't that good.

Carol   What's he doing?

Nicky   Tossing a pizza.

Carol   Oh.

Adele   We saw that done in Porto Banus.

All   Really?

Adele   Yes the chef was Spanish.

Nicky/Carol   How amazing.

Adele   They called him Carlos.

Nicky/Carol   That's interesting.

All   Waitress!!!

Mel *has entered with an imaginary pizza. The chef is Scottish.*

Mel   Can you shout up when you make a bloody order, I can't hear you. Shout up. You're bloody useless. What you think I like making pizzas in public? You must be bloody joking kiddo. This place is crap. I should have stayed on North Sea Ferries if you ask me. And the waitresses are bloody useless. (*Shouts.*) There's a steak burning here. Get your arse round here. I'll tell you what, they bring the food back all the time, I've had seafood pasta coming back here all night. What I do is this, they bring it back, all coy and helpful, I slap it in the microwave pour some sauce over it and call it a brand new dish. If they bring a steak back complaining that it's not done, I turn it over slap two bits of parsley on it, three more chips, half a tomato and it's ready to go. (*Shouts.*) Steak Diane ready to go. God. I'll tell you this, when I'm feeling really vindictive I put things from my nose in the Pizza Margarita . . . spices it up bit. One Pizza Margarita ready to go!

A sudden burst of action.

Carol Irish coffee?

Nicky Banana split?

Mel Two brandies?

Adele Seafood pasta?

Carol Steak Diane?

Mel Pizza Margarita madam . . . no no they're anchovies madam . . . yes I'm sure madam.

Carol What time is it?

Nicky Ten to.

Carol Ten to what?

Nicky Eleven.

Carol Last orders.

Mel (*comes to them*) Mario says keep serving the bastards.

Nicky Keep serving?

Mel Yeah you know what that means.

Nicky They'll stay and chat for two hours, then it's coffees and brandy till half one.

Mel And we're to send a free bottle of bubbly to whoever's birthday it is.

Carol That man is so greasy.

Nicky Hey who is that sat at table six?

Mel   Oh that's Andy King.

Nicky   Mmm very nice.

Mel   Oh no . . . too clean-looking, I only like dangerous men.

Nicky   He is dangerous.

Carol   What exactly does Steve look like, Mel? Freddy Krueger?

Mel   No, more like Rutger Hauer actually, Carol.

Nicky   Oh yes, wet your knickers.

Carol   Mmmm nice.

Mel   Who, Freddy Krueger?

Carol   Andy King.

Nicky   Carol, you man-eater.

Carol   It's an aesthetic opinion Nicky, that's all. I bet he's very aggressive, probably breast fed.

Mel   Thank you Claire Rayner.

Nicky   Mmmm very nice.

Carol   Nicky you're drooling.

Nicky   I know.

Mel   Yeah he's alright is Andy, he went to school with my cousin. She's six foot two.

Nicky   Do you know him?

Mel   I sort of know him to wink and nod at.

Carol   So you don't know him?

Mel   No, not really.

Adele (*coming to them*)   Have you seen Mario?

Mel   Yeah fat bloke, dodgy-looking.

Adele   I mean has he told you about these shorts?

Nicky   What?

Adele   He's just told me he definitely wants us in shorts, from tomorrow, he wants to see how they look.

Carol   That man is a pervert.

Adele   He says we're to try 'em because they look more trendy.

Carol   Trendy, it's so men can have a good look.

Adele   I've seen 'em, they don't look that bad.

Carol   But it's the idea of it.

Adele   They're quite smart actually.

Carol   And where is it going to lead to? It'll be shorts first and then cami-knickers and then pink tutus and then God knows what.

Nicky   Knee-high wellies?

Carol   Maybe. And fat Mario will sell more champagne and whoever's working here then will be that cheap the punters'll think a fiver will get them a blow-job.

Mel   I'd do it for twenty. I was joking. I wouldn't do it for a thousand.

Nicky   Dunno?

Adele   Well we'll see what happens tomorrow then won't we. Because I've got a kid to feed Carol. I can't afford not to do wht I'm told.

Carol   So you'll wear 'em then?

Adele   Yeah, and I might stick a flower up my arse and all.

Carol   You're being selfish.

Adele   No I'm not.

Nicky   I don't want anything to do with it, me.

Adele   Well you're lucky aren't you?

Nicky   Yeah I am yeah, and I've worked bloody hard for it.

Adele   Oh have you.

Nicky   Yes I bloody have.

Mel   Listen I'm wearing no shorts or nothing, but be honest Carol when we went out on Nicky's birthday you wore a dress that was that short I could see your breakfast.

Adele   Yeah you did.

Nicky   You've got nice legs.

Carol   That was different.

Mel   Was it?

Carol   I was wearing that for me.

Mel   So you're not bothered about men looking at your legs when you want them to?

Carol   Going out for a meal is different isn't it. You're not on show. You're not seducing the punters' fantasies.

Mel   You what?

Carol   I'll tell you this, if you wear them shorts tomorrow, I'll rip 'em off you.

Nicky   Oh you kinky bitch Carol.

Adele   Oh yeah?

Carol   Yes I mean it Adele.

Adele   I'm sorry Carol, I am, honest. I don't want all this to happen, and I'm not thick. I know what you're on about.

Carol   I do mean it. If you wear those shorts Adele, you're dropping us all in it. You just think about it ... .

Adele (*suddenly turning into another tone*)   Can you finish your drinks off now please.

Nicky   Thank you ladies and gents, time to go home.

Carol   Time please.

Mel   Twenty-one? Yeah happy birthday.

Nicky   I wonder if Vicky's burnt the meal. There's always somebody worse off than you are just think about that.

Adele   I hope you freeze to death in Norway.

Nicky   You don't do you?

Adele   No ... no I don't ...

Mel   Have you seen the toilets?

Carol   What about 'em.

Mel   It's like the Black Hole of Calcutta; you can't move for hair spray.

Blackout. Lights up. Toilets. **Nicky** *still sniffing.*

Nicky   So she says to me if you don't keep your bloody hands off him I'll slap you.

Mel   Did she? She must have seen us waving at him.

Nicky   As if I'm scared of her.

Carol   She's a fart, you can tell from her handbag.

Nicky   I don't know what he sees in her.

Adele   I don't.

Nicky   And I thought it was going to all work out tonight.

Mel   We've had a good time anyway haven't we?

Nicky   I suppose so.

Adele   Course we have. Who needs Andy King anyway?

Nicky   But I love him.

Carol   You don't, you're drunk. She's drunk everybody just ignore her. God these mirrors really show up your spots.

Nicky   And I feel embarrassed.

Adele   Hey look have I gone pale?

Carol   I wish I had.

Nicky   I'll kill our Sandra for telling me lies.

Mel   Can I borrow your comb?

Carol   Yes here. My hair's dropped.

Adele   It suits you like that.

Carol   What? A mess?

Adele   No, that style.

Carol (*as if lifting up her skirt*)   Here, have you seen this? I've got loads of cellulite.

Mel   I have.

Adele   I can't see any.

Carol   You can if you squeeze my bum.

Adele   Oh yeah! Sago pudding!

Carol   Is it that bad? That's it, I'm going to start doing my callanetics again.

Nicky   I've got cellulite, that's probably why he doesn't like me.

Mel   As if he can see it through your dress.

Nicky I bet she's not got it, her he's with, she looks like a soddin' model.

Carol She looks like a tart. Have you got any hair spray?

Adele I have, there's just a bit left.

Mel Do them callanetics work?

Carol Yes they're brilliant. You can lose a stone in half a day.

Nicky Do you think she's nicer-looking than me?

Adele Look, have a few more drinks and forget about it. It's your birthday, it's not every week that you're twenty-one!

Nicky I just want to die.

Mel It's them Bloody Marys, they're bloody lethal.

Carol I'm going to have another.

Mel Well I've gone all dizzy.

Adele Don't be sick.

Nicky You know something. I hate my face.

Carol Put a bag on your head!

Nicky Ooooaah . . .

Music. We're no longer in the toilets. **Carol**, **Adele**, **Nicky** *and* **Mel** *are reflecting on the last scene.*

Adele There's another girl crying in the toilets.

Nicky Oh well.

Adele Over a man.

Carol Pathetic.

Nicky Who is it?

Adele Somebody, Andy King I think.

Nicky   Oh well.

Mel   Is she drunk?

Adele   Looks like it.

Carol   Ruled by their heads and not their hearts.

Mel   They're only having a good time.

Carol   Are they?

Adele   Yes they are.

Carol   Well I suppose if that's all they've got to look forward to . . .

Nicky   What?

Adele   Sometimes Carol you're depressing.

Mel   Yeah at least they're looking for a man Carol, and not just taking photos of them.

All (*sarcastic reaction*)   Ooooooohhhhhh.

The 'oooohhh' becomes the conga. They begin to conga around the stage.

Na na na na na na – na,
We're getting very drunk now
We're getting very merry
Happy birthday Elaine,
What a super party.

Adele   I've got a silly hat on . . .

Nicky   I've ruined my mascara . . .

Mel   I've laddered all my stockings . . .

Carol   I've stuffed my face quite stupid . . .

All   Na, na, na, na. Na, na, na, na . . .

Gradually the noise fades as does the dance and the conga is replaced with the four supermarket girls just outside Shakers Bar.
Nicky (*Elaine*) *is still very tearful.*

Nicky　I feel sick.

Adele　You're right.

Mel　I feel fine now.

Nicky　Everything's spinning round.

Carol　What time is it?

Nicky　Honestly, I think I'm going to faint.

Carol　Go home then, 'cos I'll tell you sommat, you're getting on my nerves.

Nicky　I can't go home, it's my birthday.

Adele　Why don't we go to a disco?

Mel　A club?

Adele　Yeah.

Carol　Brilliant. I could go on all night.

Nicky　Everything's ruined, nobody cares, nobody's bothered . . .

Carol　Oh stop crying will you, it's been like being with Gazza for the last two hours.

Nicky　It's you, you don't know what it's like to be in love.

Carol　In love? Isn't that supposed to make you happy?

Adele　It can hurt though Trace.

Nicky　Yeah well it's hurting me now. I've got this awful pain in my chest.

Carol　It's indigestion.

Mel　Or your bra's too tight.

Adele　Too many anchovies early on.

Nicky　It's not. It's Andy King. He's my perfect man,

I know it. It's just that he doesn't realise.

Adele Come off it, you've never even spoke.

Nicky I have, I have . . .

Mel When?

Nicky At work, when I was on cereals, he came up and asked me where the Ready Brek was.

Adele Who wants a man who eats Ready Brek?

Nicky I do . . . I do . . .

Carol Oh for God's sake.

Mel It's alright Elaine love, come on, there'll be loads of nice blokes down the disco.

Nicky I'm not bothered.

Carol Look, you've got to accept it, he doesn't like you, he's got a girlfriend and he doesn't like you!

Mel Don't.

Adele I think men are overrated. I always have a better time on my own.

Mel Is it starting to rain?

Carol Shit, come on let's leg it to Pinocchio's.

Nicky I don't want to.

Adele Cheer up Elaine, you're only twenty-one once, you want to remember it as being happy.

Nicky I can't.

Carol Oh leave her, she's a pain in the neck.

Mel I'm getting wet through.

Adele Come on love.

Nicky I don't want . . .

Carol   Leave her . . .

Mel   We can't . . .

Adele   She's pathetic . . .

Carol   Leave her . . .

Mel   Oh alright . . . Thanks for the meal Elaine. My steak wasn't cooked, but it was lovely.

Adele   Yes thanks, it was lovely.

Carol   You'll be alright, get yourself a taxi.

Nicky   Aooh . . .

Mel   See you tomorrow.

Adele   Is it far this disco?

Carol   Not really.

Adele   See you, take care . . .

Nicky   Aaaoooh . . .

Mel   Are you sure she's going to be alright?

Carol   Look I don't care, she's driving me absolutely insane. I've heard there's a nice DJ at Pinocchio's.

Mel   There is . . .

Carol   He's gorgeous, Bruno they call him.

Adele   Brilliant! Let's get going then!

All Three   Yeahhh!

Nicky (*shouting after them*)   Hey! I've changed my mind, I think I might come with you! Hey! . . . Wait for me! . . . It's my birthday remember . . . Wait! . . . you bastards . . . Wait.

Lights. We are back in Shakers. The girls are bidding a number of clients good night.

Adele   Good night.

Nicky Ta-ra.

Mel See you again.

Carol Drive carefully . . .

Adele Take care.

All Good night!

Nicky That's it then.

Carol Turn that bloody music off.

Mel Yeah let's have a bit of peace and quiet.

Nicky Oh I quite like it.

Adele I'm going to get off . . .

Mel I think the air-conditioning's come on.

Carol Oh great.

Adele I'll see you then shall I?

Mel Look at the mess . . .

Nicky Somebody's left their scarf.

Adele Is it OK?

Nicky Just go Adele.

Adele Right . . .

Carol And think about tomorrow . . .

Adele I will.

Nicky Go . . . or you'll miss the bus . . .

Adele Thanks.

Carol Go on . . .

Adele Hey you can have my tips.

Nicky Brilliant.

Carol Look at her . . .

Adele   See you then . . .

Mel   Adele get. Go on. Shoooo . . .

Silence. **Adele** *stops, turns to the audience. In spotlight.*

Adele   You know at times like these I feel like they
hate me for having Emma. I hate myself for having
Emma. I hate Emma, I know, I shouldn't say things
like that, but I have feelings inside that I don't know
how to cope with because they're all mixed up with
other feelings of love. You see right at this moment
I've had enough, I don't want to get the bus, I don't
want to walk up the estate. I don't want to pick up
this sleeping thing and wheel her home, hoping she
doesn't cry. I want just to be able to think about me,
to watch the late-night film on the telly and relax with
a glass of wine. But I know that when I see her, her
hair all floppy, I feel a love so strong, so like nothing
else that it makes me glad to be alive. But I've got to
stick at it until she starts school. Then it's got to
change, for the sake of both of us. Do you know what
I'd really like? To . . . work in a travel agent's, sending
lots of people to the sun. I'd get home early and
Emma will run in from school and we'll laugh and
look at her paintings. Maybe then I'll see my life in
colour instead of black and white.

Adele *exits. Silence. Lights back to the bar.*

Mel   I think I might go early tomorrow.

Carol   Fine.

Mel   About half eight OK?

Nicky   Yeah, I'll go early Monday.

Carol   That music is ringing in my head.

Nicky   Turn it back on . . .

Carol   Some nights I can't get to sleep because of the
songs going round and round. I wake up the next day

and I'm suddenly singing the lyrics to 'I Want to Sex You Up'.

Mel   Look at the mess in here, it's like an elephant's been sick.

Nicky   Where?

Mel   Table four . . .

Nicky   Oh yeah . . . seafood pasta.

Carol   My back's killing me . . .

Mel   Innit quiet . . .

Carol   I've got neckache . . .

Nicky   Yeah it is.

Carol   My feet are killing me . . .

Nicky   Somebody coming . . .

Carol (*noticing a member of the audience, a punter*)   Sorry we're closed, closed, read my lips. If you can read. Closed.

Nicky   You should have come earlier.

Carol   They're trying to get a last drink.

Nicky   It's because the lights are on.

Carol   Closed sorry. No I can't sorry.

Nicky   They won't listen. Look at 'em, they're pissed up anyway.

Mel *walks to the spot.*

Carol   You tell 'em Mel, I'm shagged out.

Nicky   Carol.

Carol (*to audience*)   Sorry.

Mel   Oi fuck off we're shut! (*To the others.*) They're going. I think they got the message.

Adele *who has been stood upstage, joins the others as the lights fade to night. The four stand as at the beginning.*

Adele And then the long walk home. Your footsteps resound through the night. And you are alone in the dark. Alone in the night.

Carol All is dark, the pavestones are wet with the sweat of the night.

Mel And as you walk, shadows in doorways, noises around corners. Coming towards you, two dark figures.

Nicky Should you run. Oh God they're coming straight for you. You freeze to the spot.

All Good night love . . . ha ha . . . d'you wanna come to a party . . .

Carol No.

All No thanks.

Carol I've just been to one. We are Carol.

Adele Adele.

Nicky Nicky.

Mel And Mel.

All
And we work in a bar that is worse than hell.
And we serve the drinks and we serve the food.
We have to be nice,
Not ever be rude.
So no matter what you do,
No matter what you say,
It's a happy smiling face . . .
That comes your way.

The actresses smile and freeze. The Housemartins' 'Happy Hour' plays. There is a slow fade to black.

Methuen Contemporary Dramatists
include

Peter Barnes (three volumes)
Sebastian Barry
Dermot Bolger
Edward Bond (six volumes)
Howard Brenton
  (two volumes)
Richard Cameron
Jim Cartwright
Caryl Churchill (two volumes)
Sarah Daniels (two volumes)
Nick Darke
David Edgar (three volumes)
Ben Elton
Dario Fo (two volumes)
Michael Frayn (two volumes)
Paul Godfrey
John Guare
Peter Handke
Jonathan Harvey
Declan Hughes
Terry Johnson (two volumes)
Bernard-Marie Koltès
David Lan
Bryony Lavery
Doug Lucie
David Mamet (three volumes)

Martin McDonagh
Duncan McLean
Anthony Minghella
  (two volumes)
Tom Murphy (four volumes)
Phyllis Nagy
Anthony Nielsen
Philip Osment
Louise Page
Stewart Parker (two volumes)
Joe Penhall
Stephen Poliakoff
  (three volumes)
Christina Reid
Philip Ridley
Willy Russell
Ntozake Shange
Sam Shepard (two volumes)
Wole Soyinka (two volumes)
David Storey (three volumes)
Sue Townsend
Michel Vinaver (two volumes)
Michael Wilcox
David Wood (two volumes)
Victoria Wood

Methuen World Classics
include

Jean Anouilh (two volumes)
John Arden (two volumes)
Arden & D'Arcy
Brendan Behan
Aphra Behn
Bertolt Brecht (six volumes)
Büchner
Bulgakov
Calderón
Čapek
Anton Chekhov
Noel Coward (seven volumes)
Eduardo De Filippo
Max Frisch
John Galsworthy
Gogol
Gorky
Harley Granville Barker
  (two volumes)
Henrik Ibsen (six volumes)
Lorca (three volumes)

Marivaux
Mustapha Matura
David Mercer (two volumes)
Arthur Miller (five volumes)
Molière
Musset
Peter Nichols (two volumes)
Clifford Odets
Joe Orton
A. W. Pinero
Luigi Pirandello
Terence Rattigan
  (two volumes)
W. Somerset Maugham
  (two volumes)
August Strindberg
  (three volumes)
J. M. Synge
Ramón del Valle-Inclán
Frank Wedekind
Oscar Wilde

Methuen Modern Plays
include work by

Jean Anouilh
John Arden
Margaretta D'Arcy
Peter Barnes
Sebastian Barry
Brendan Behan
Dermot Bolger
Edward Bond
Bertolt Brecht
Howard Brenton
Anthony Burgess
Simon Burke
Jim Cartwright
Caryl Churchill
Noël Coward
Lucinda Coxon
Sarah Daniels
Nick Darke
Nick Dear
Shelagh Delaney
David Edgar
David Eldridge
Dario Fo
Michael Frayn
John Godber
Paul Godfrey
David Greig
John Guare
Peter Handke
David Harrower
Jonathan Harvey
Iain Heggie
Declan Hughes
Terry Johnson
Sarah Kane
Charlotte Keatley
Barrie Keeffe
Howard Korder

Robert Lepage
Stephen Lowe
Doug Lucie
Martin McDonagh
John McGrath
Terrence McNally
David Mamet
Patrick Marber
Arthur Miller
Mtwa, Ngema & Simon
Tom Murphy
Phyllis Nagy
Peter Mtwa
Joseph O'Connor
Joe Orton
Louise Page
Joe Penhall
Luigi Pirandello
Stephen Poliakoff
Franca Rame
Mark Ravenhill
Philip Ridley
Reginald Rose
David Rudkin
Willy Russell
Jean-Paul Sartre
Sam Shepard
Wole Soyinka
Shelagh Stephenson
C. P. Taylor
Theatre de Complicite
Theatre Workshop
Sue Townsend
Judy Upton
Timberlake Wertenbaker
Roy Williams
Victoria Wood

For a Complete Catalogue of Methuen Drama titles
write to:

Methuen Drama
215 Vauxhall Bridge Road
London SW1V 1EJ

or you can visit our website at:

www.methuen.co.uk